The Executive Coach in the Corporate Forest

A Business Fable

Steve Gladis, Ph.D.

Foreword by
Marshall Goldsmith

D1603841

HRD Press, Inc. • Amherst • Massachusetts

Disclaimer

This is a work of fiction. All names, characters, places, and incidents are the product of the author's imagination or are used fictionally. Any resemblance to actual persons — living or dead — businesses, companies, organizations, events, or locales is entirely coincidental.

Published by: HRD Press, Inc.
22 Amherst Road
Amherst, Massachusetts 01002
1-800-822-2801 (U.S. and Canada)
1-413-253-3488
1-413-253-3490 (fax)
http://www.hrdpress.com

ISBN: 978-1-59996-130-9

Editorial services by Sally M. Farnham
Production services by Anctil Virtual Office
Cover design by Eileen Klockars

This book is dedicated to Marshall Goldsmith, who is arguably the best executive coach in the country. I offer my most sincere gratitude for his teaching and writing, which have guided my own executive coaching and that of so many others.

Contents

Foreword

Executive coaching has come of age, and it's been my great privilege to have been a part of its growth. As such, I've been honored to have worked with more than 80 CEOs in the world's top corporations and helped implement leadership development processes that have impacted more than one million people. During that time, I've learned that great leadership is a journey—simply put, a journey from here to there. But what got you here won't necessarily get you there. In fact, my newest book is entitled just that: *What Got You Here Won't Get You There.*

One of the difficulties with executive coaching is explaining it to executives who don't understand the process that coaches employ to get people from here to there. Some executives think that coaching is all about an executive coach telling them what to do, and they will be somehow magically "fixed." Actually, great coaches ask far more probing questions than they give exact answers or directions—which differentiates them from subject-matter-expert consultants. While great coaches are experts at the coaching process of change, they don't give you all the answers, rather they help you discover the best path for yourself and ensure that you stay on the path . . . getting from here to there.

That's why I like what Steve Gladis has done with *The Executive Coach in the Corporate Forest.* Steve has offered a clear window into the profession to corporate leaders, human resource managers, and those interested in understanding the journey of executive coaching. He has written an immensely readable business fable (a fictional case study). Anyone who has read and enjoyed other best-selling business fables such as Patrick Lencioni's popular *The Five Dysfunctions of a Team* or Spencer Johnson and Ken Blanchard's *Who Moved My Cheese?* will most certainly enjoy *The Executive Coach in the Corporate Forest.*

It's the story of a young, gifted executive coach, J.C. Williams, and his coaching relationships with his rather varied and fascinating business clients — all with their own professional challenges. The book offers engaging stories, has believable characters with realistic problems, illustrates the structure and content of the coaching process, and has been vetted by other executive coaches, including me. The book is a quick read — something any busy CEO or executive could read on a flight between Boston and Chicago — time very well spent, not only for the individual executive but for his or her company's future.

Why is this book important?

When executives realize that they need assistance to get to the next level, to solve a problem, or to alter a behavior that has stalled their career development, they need to make a change. As one humorist once said, "The definition of insanity is doing the same thing over and over again expecting different results."

Many executives have heard about executive coaching but don't know what it actually looks like. Through this book, *The Executive Coach in the Corporate Forest,* Steve Gladis has given such inquiring executives a clear picture of the entire executive coaching process from start to finish. I enjoyed all the characters with their own quirks and issues, many of which I've seen in my own Fortune 500 clients. Steve has done an outstanding job, and the next time someone asks me what executive coaching is all about, I'll say, "Just read *The Executive Coach in the Corporate Forest.*"

— Marshall Goldsmith

Marshall Goldsmith is America's preeminent executive coach. His clients represent some of the country's leading corporations and institutions. The American Management Association recently named Marshall one of the 50 great thinkers and business leaders who have impacted the field of management, and *Business Week* listed him as one of the most influential practitioners in the history of leadership development. He serves on the faculty of Dartmouth College's Tuck School of Business and has authored 23 books. Marshall's newest book, *What Got You Here Won't Get You There,* is a *New York Times* bestseller and a *Wall Street Journal* #1 business book.

Preface

You're about to read a business fable, which is a fictional business case study. In this fable, I've tried to demonstrate the theory and practice of the executive coaching process. Because of the confidential nature of coaching, I created fictional characters with realistic problems so that readers, including potential coaching clients, could see and understand what good executive coaching looks like in different situations, from both the client's and the executive coach's perspectives.

I have found that many people don't have an accurate picture of executive coaching. Consequently they are often confused and sometimes disappointed by their unrealistic expectations, such as wanting the coach to simply give them the answers to their problems. Clients constantly confuse executive coaching with consulting (where experts *are* hired to provide business solutions) or counseling (where trained counselors *are* expected to probe the past to find a better path to the future).

Executive coaching (where coaches are trusted to use positive inquiry and questions to help clients understand their current issues) is neither consulting nor counseling. When clients get a firm handle on what executive coaching can and cannot do, they and their coaches are off to a much better start.

So, I created this story about J.C. Williams, a young, intelligent, and talented executive coach who is wise beyond his years because of his own life story. In the book, you'll meet a host of characters, including Allison Centarus and Liz Penrith, two of J.C.'s special friends and colleagues who act as his sounding boards. You'll also meet an array of clients, all with varying issues: Stuart Samuelsson, the gruff CEO with some serious personal and professional problems; Ann Tabor, an executive who is loved by everyone but who has a tough time saying "No"; Jane Smithfield, a brilliant, technical COO whose interpersonal skills need honing before her CEO will let her take the company's reins; David Blackmon, a tall, handsome community foundation leader with a big ego to match, referred to coaching by a concerned chairperson; Jonathan Jeffries, a brilliant surgeon with a vindictive streak, who is referred to coaching by the administrator at the hospital where he practices. You'll also meet Big Walt, J.C.'s now-deceased father, whose memory sustains J.C. through his own personal trials and whose wisdom guides J.C.'s coaching practice. I hope you enjoy this cast of characters and your journey into the world of executive coaching.

Finally, Chapter 22 (What Is Executive Coaching?) serves as a capstone for the fable. I use it to explain the theory and practice of executive coaching in more depth and refer back to the text for specific examples and linkages. My fondest wish is that the process of executive coaching becomes clearer and that more people will use the service to help them reach their goals and objectives, as well as to make themselves (and their businesses) more effective and efficient—and ultimately healthier and happier.

Chapter 1:
One Hardwood Tree

"Marie, get Jack in here, right now," Stuart Samuelsson said.
   "Yes, sir."
   Fifty-something, graying, tall, and angular, Stuart sat in his 30th-floor corner office at a mahogany desk, described by one of his senior executives as "large enough to land a small aircraft on." This office had been the whipping shed for many an executive in the past, as Samuelsson Technology had risen from a small technology reseller into a major systems integrator and government contractor.
   Jack Wilhelm knocked on the door frame outside Stuart's office, guarded ferociously by Marie Collingwood. "Stuart, you wanted to see me?"
   Still bearing down on the spreadsheet in front of him, peering through the lens of his bifocals rather than raising his head to acknowledge his visitor, Stuart motioned Jack into one of the two leather wing chairs in front of his desk—and not toward the conversation nook in the corner.
   "These numbers look awful," Stuart said.
   "Let me explain for a minute."
   "We're down 5 percent this quarter."
   "I'm aware, but—"
   "But nothing. Get these numbers pointed north or give me a plan to start cutting back personnel—starting with your department."
   "Stuart. Listen. I . . ."
   Stuart took off his glasses and tossed them on his desk. "I'm done listening. For the past two quarters you've told me about the competitive market, the global economy, the whatever. I want results, not excuses, Jack—now." He gestured toward the door.

That evening when Stuart arrived home, he threw his keys onto the table, opened the refrigerator, took out a beer, and sat at the table looking over the day's mail. When his wife, Angela, walked in, he was reading the MasterCard bill that listed scores of items for three pages. She came toward him to give him a kiss, but he looked at her with the bill in hand and said, "What the hell did you buy for $1,000?"

"What are you talking about?"

He pointed to the charge and said, "You have to stop your compulsive shopping."

"My what?"

"You're spending money like a drunken sailor."

"You're incredible. I bought you that special mattress for your back. It was going to be a surprise."

"You have to control your spending."

"Have you listened to yourself lately, Stuart? You sound more like a financial analyst than a husband."

"And you spend money with all the responsibility of a teenager."

"I'm not listening to this conversation," she said and walked out of the house toward the backyard.

The following day when Stuart arrived at his desk, he found an e-mail message from his best friend, Randy Moore, someone he'd known at the Harvard Business School.

Sending a friend to see you at 3:00 p.m. today. Listen to him. He's one of the best executive coaches in the business. I used him and think you need to talk to him. Trust me on this one, buddy. No need to reply.

—Randy

Stuart started to hit "Reply," then just deleted the message.

About 3:00 that afternoon, Marie buzzed Stuart's line. "There's a J.C. Williams here to see you," she said. "Says he has an appointment, but I have nothing on the calendar. He mentioned Randy Moore."

"Tell him . . ." Stuart started to say but then caught himself. "Give me 10 to 15 minutes to finish what I'm working on. Send him in at about 3:15."

"Certainly."

A quarter-hour later, a slender young man in jeans, a blue blazer, and an open shirt, maybe in his mid-to-late thirties, walked into Stuart's office and sat in the conversation area in a large chair.

At first, Samuelsson stared and said nothing, but eventually he stood up and walked over to the young man. Without extending his hand, he said, "I'm Stuart Samuelsson. How can I help you?"

J.C. looked around, studying the office—more a monument, he thought, than an office—full of civic, business, and personal awards and trophies.

Stuart sat down on the couch and looked at J.C. "Look, son, I'm a very busy man," he said. "I know you're a friend of Randy's. That's what got you in here."

J.C. looked at him as he tilted his head curiously, as if that would help him understand better.

"Well?"

"Can I ask you a question?" J.C. said.

"Depends."

"On what?"

"The nature of the question."

"So, what are those boundaries?"

"Look. Just ask your question," Stuart said, with a cold stare at J.C.

"What would most people say is your strongest character strength?"

"What?" Stuart said. He lifted off his glasses, almost like he was preparing for a fight.

"You told me to ask the question."

"This is inappropriate." And Stuart waved his hand, dismissing J.C. along with the question.

"Why?"

"I don't know you, you're a kid, I'm busy," he answered, now looking back at the pile of papers on his desk that he desperately wanted to get back to.

"But you know and trust Randy?"

"Yes."

"So can't you give me the benefit of the doubt?" J.C. said. He stared at Stuart.

Stuart looked at his watch and said, "Look I'm pressed. What was your question again?"

"What would most people say is your strongest character strength?"

Stuart thought for a few seconds and answered, "My intelligence."

"That you're a smart guy?"

"I suppose you could put it that way."

"How so?"

"I understand how business works. Profit, loss, markets, economics . . . I'm a bottom-line guy."

"And would you agree with their assessment—you're a smart guy?"

"Yes. I'd say that's accurate."

"Smart. Not a bad thing to be known for."

Stuart almost smiled.

"Smart in other ways?"

"What other ways?"

"In relationships?"

Stuart hesitated before he answered. "With people?"

"Yes, how would they say you understand people— apart from your business skills?"

"Well, they'd say, I'm . . ." he paused to think. "Honest—direct."

"So, smart and honest. Pretty impressive. What does being honest look like at work?"

"Telling people the truth, even when it's uncomfortable."

"OK. For example?"

"Honest feedback. Telling people when they're not hitting the mark. Telling them exactly what they need to hear—not what they want to hear."

J.C. got up and walked over to the tall, glass-covered bookcase and looked at the plaques, crystal vases, and other mementos and awards bearing Stuart Samuelsson's name. He studied them and then turned back to Stuart.

"An impressive collection of awards. I'm wondering which one of these you're the most proud of?"

Stuart rose and walked over to the bookcase, thought for a few moments, and pointed deep into the bottom corner at a baseball. "That one."

"Why?"

"We won the league that year, and I pitched the final game."

"So winning an important game is significant to you."

"Yes."

"What else?"

"Look I don't have time for this. What do you want?"

"Randy thought we should meet. I can come back another time, if that's better for you?"

"Look, I can have you talk to our HR department if you're looking for coaching clients."

"I'm not looking for more clients."

"Then what?"

"Just determining if I would want to work with you."

"Being more than presumptuous, aren't you?"

"Perhaps a bit, but I was under the impression that you and Randy spoke. If I'm mistaken, I can see myself out."

"Probably a good idea."

With that, J.C. started toward the door. Just as he was about to leave, he turned and said, "One last question?"

Stuart had returned to his desk and put his glasses back on, then looked up. "What?"

"One final question?"

"Fine," he said, his voice on edge.

"Why do you like to win?"

"Look, I'm just too busy. Good day."

Over the next couple of weeks, J.C.'s question floated in and out of Stuart's brain while he worked ferociously to turn around the company's financial situation. He rode Jack and his team hard, and the numbers began to point north again.

Then one afternoon, Jack came into Stuart's office and announced that he'd just taken a new job as the CEO of a smaller but growing company. It was a great opportunity that just seemed to come his way. "Serendipity" was the word he used. No, it was not about the pay at Samuelsson and no, not about the pressure on the numbers. It was an opportunity he could not pass up—or so Jack claimed. A month later, two of Jack's key managers also resigned and joined Jack at his new company.

A few days before he had gotten the two latest resignations, Stuart had received—and ignored—a note that J.C. had called. Now he was ready to respond.

"Marie, get J.C. Williams on the phone for me," he said on the intercom.

Two days later they met at a local Starbucks. When J.C. shook his hand and asked him how he was, Stuart said simply, "OK."

"That bad?"

"I've thought about your question."

"About winning?"

"Yes, partly," Stuart said, looking out the window and collecting his thoughts.

"What's the other part?"

"Well, the coach who gave me that ball was a great guy. The reason I pitched in college and almost went to the pros."

"Tell me about him," J.C. responded as he leaned toward the CEO.

"Rob Thresh, Big Rob, we used to call him. He was a hardware store salesman who coached his kid's baseball teams all through school," Stuart said while his face relaxed and a faint smile darted across his face if only for a second.

"Knew a lot about baseball?"

"Not as much as most coaches in the league. It was more about how he coached."

"What'd he do?"

"More about *how* he did it. He never told you what you were doing wrong. Always focused on what you were doing right—went from there."

"Can you give me an example?"

"Once in a game I started pitching wild. He came out to the mound, put his arm around me and said, 'You have a hell of a great arm—just stare at the catcher's glove and forget the batter.' Then, he went back to the dugout. I struck out the next two batters, and we won."

"So, what do you think happened?"

"I'd lost confidence. And Rob knew just what to say."

"What do you figure would have happened if he'd said, 'Stop screwing up, or I'll take you out'?"

"I'd have probably fallen apart on the mound and gotten even wilder."

"So, what does that tell you about your own managing style?"

"Business is different. We're not playing a game. It's bottom-line stuff."

"Really? How do you conclude that?"

"Here we go again with the questions."

"OK then, may I have your permission to make an observation?"

"Yeah. Shoot."

"You told me on the phone that you just lost three key executives."

"They left for other opportunities."

"That's what they told you," J.C. said. "I'd submit that if your old coach had raked you over the coals every time you had a bad game, you'd eventually have quit the team. Is that a fair assessment — yes or no?"

Stuart thought for a moment, and then in a softer voice said, "Yes."

"So why would your executives be any different?"

"We're not talking about children here. These are grown men."

"Oh, really?"

"Come on, for God's sake."

"Then, please tell me why you've kept that ball in your trophy cabinet all these years."

"I . . . Well, it's just a . . . well . . . a memento."

"Again. If I may offer an opinion?"

"Stop with the permission stuff. Speak your mind."

"OK, thank you. I'd say that the ball is far more than a memento—it's a symbol of the best boss you ever worked for. But you've forgotten the lesson he taught and stuck it on the bottom shelf of your memory."

"This is psycho mumbo jumbo."

"Fair enough, but I have only one last question and then I'll shut up."

"Fine with me."

"If your old coach saw you managing your company, what do you think he'd say?"

Stuart stared at J.C., then at the floor, then at his coffee. But before he could answer, J.C. stood up and said, "Don't tell me now. Think about it and call me in a few weeks if you still want to talk."

Stuart just sat there and kept staring at his coffee.

Chapter 2:
The Path Not Taken

J.C. walked into his office and headed right for the black faculty rocking chair that he'd been given when he chose to leave the prestigious Darden Business School faculty at the University of Virginia. At age 33, Associate Professor John Cameron "J.C." Williams had become one of the youngest associates at Darden and was enormously popular with faculty and students alike. In fact, his five years at the business school had been the most rewarding time in his short life. He'd managed to write two books and a host of articles in his field of choice, business communications, for which he'd been recognized by nearly every major journal as a rising academic star.

His relationships with the students had bordered on cultism. Young and energetic, the blue-jeaned, sandy-haired professor drew the admiration of all his students and filled more than a few daydreams of the women on staff and in his classes. He was clearly on a superstar's glide path when he found a lump under his left breast one day while he was taking a shower. At first it felt like a cyst of some sort, which he ignored for a month or so. Then it began to become tender to the touch, so J.C. went to his doctor at the University's hospital to have it checked out.

The doctor's voice was reverent and steady when he announced the biopsy results to J.C. "Stage 3 lymphoma," he said. "We'll need to operate and then do radiation and chemo."

That day changed J.C.'s view of the world forever.

He'd remembered his father telling him that certain life experiences take you on a new path—perhaps not one you may have chosen. His father, Walt, for example, had survived being a second lieutenant in Vietnam, and then decided to become a journalist, " . . . to tell the truth about life" as best he could. An overweight, soft-spoken, stoic man, Walt had not been one to talk much about Vietnam, even though J.C. had prodded him endlessly. The few stories he had been able to tease out always ended with Walt's caveat about war — "man at his worst." Now he told J.C., "We'll get through this, son. We will."

For J.C., that year of diagnosis, surgery, chemo, radiation, sickness, and fatigue allowed him time to reflect on his own life. The University had been wonderful and granted J.C. extended leave with full pay, which allowed him to live with his parents as he went through the ordeal.

His recovery from the surgery had gone well, with some minor complications involving his left arm, but this was almost unnoticeable unless he was doing something strenuous. However, the aspiration he'd had in college — to be a professional baseball pitcher — seemed ludicrous these days, even in retrospect. He used to have a wicked curve that drove right-handed batters crazy and won him All-American status his senior year at Stanford. Had it not been for winning a Rhodes Scholarship to study at Oxford, he would have gladly taken one of the dozen offers he had gotten from the pros. In the end, he had followed Walt's advice — given only after J.C. badgered him to offer it. Walt had asked, "What do you want to do?"

"Both of them."

"So do them."

"But I have to choose," J.C. said, and he hit the table with his hand — a little harder than he had intended.

Walt didn't move, just leaned in toward his son and said, "Do you?"

"Of course!" J.C. blurted in frustration.

"Why can't you do them both?"

"How so?" J.C. asked, stunned by the question.

"How long is the Rhodes commitment for?"

"A year."

"Will that affect the offers?"

"Some, but not much as long as I don't get hurt in England."

"I suppose that means if you don't get stabbed with a pen."

J.C. had laughed and then thought about the conversation until the deadline for the Rhodes acceptance. Ultimately he decided to go to England and then to get his MBA and Ph.D. at Harvard. He never regretted the decision.

On August 15th, J.C. made another big decision in his life—not to return to UVa's Darden School of Business to teach for the fall. Giving up a tenured professor's position at such an early age, and at such an excellent institution, was not just an anomaly, but perhaps a rarity.

"I'm not sure if I should go back to the University or not," J.C. said, running his hand through his sandy hair.

"I'd say it's up to you."

"But what do you think?" J.C. asked, with an edge to his voice.

"It's a choice only you can make. How do you feel about it?"

"Confused, frustrated."

"How so?"

"I've read and written so many case studies, I feel like a bit of an actor when I teach."

"Why?"

"I'm detached from reality in a way. Surrounded by bricks and columns while real businessmen and women are out there doing it."

"So, do you want to get a job in some company? Is that it?"

"Not exactly, but that's the idea. Practice what I preach — at least for a while."

"What company do you think you'd most like to work for?"

J.C. hesitated before he answered because he knew how unassuming and humble his father was. What he was about to say to a guy who had worked for the same newspaper for 35 years might sound presumptuous. But the words finally came.

"I think I'd like to start my own firm."

"Doing what?" Walt asked without batting an eye.

"Coaching executives."

"That way you get both your dreams."

"What? How so?"

"Athletics and business."

"Oh! Now I see. Well, it's a lot different in some ways, but similar in other ways."

That was the day J.C. Williams, LLC, was born.

Now, several years later, J.C. had opened an office in a business incubator — the Mason Enterprise Center — run by George Mason University (GMU), just off its campus in Fairfax, Virginia. He had built his business centered on senior executives in the Greater Metropolitan Washington and Northern Virginia region and had grown his business to nearly a million dollars a year in revenues, with only minor expenses — his office and a part-time assistant, a GMU graduate student.

But as small as his company was, he was in demand by some of the biggest companies in the region, which had been referred to him by his colleagues at the University — his best salespeople. Also, a number of larger firms from New York and DC had tried to buy his firm and him — more for him than his clients. He'd been interviewed by both *Forbes* and *Fortune* as the wunderkind of executive coaching.

Now in his fifth year of business, J.C. had rebuffed attempts to get rich quick by selling his company. And he always sought the wise counsel of his own personal executive coach, Big Walt.

And all Walt ever advised was for J.C. to do what he loved.

"That's where you'll get your energy," Walt had told him over the years. So J.C. used that advice to light his path when he got in a dark place or confused by a world crowding in on him.

During that fifth year, when he thought his firm had "made it" by all the usual business-success tests, J.C. had to undergo a new personal challenge. That year, Big Walt died suddenly of a heart attack. The shock of Walt's loss had been enormous, for J.C. and for his mother. J.C. took three months off to take care of his parents' financial affairs. Walt's death further etched on J.C.'s heart the importance of doing what he wanted, not what others wanted or expected.

Chapter 3:
The Willow in the Woods

J.C. got the call from Leo Farnelli, CEO at SameTech1, a billion-dollar-a-year systems integrator for the federal government. Leo cleared his throat and asked, "J.C., you ever meet someone who's too nice?"

"What do you mean?"

"I have an executive who's, well, just too nice. I mean everyone loves her."

"And that's a bad thing?"

"No. Not if you think of it in only one way."

"So help me understand it the way that you're thinking of it."

"I'll give you an example. Ann, that's her name, Ann Tabor."

"Anne Taylor, like the clothing company?

"No, Tabor, T-A-B-O-R."

"Oh, sorry."

"She runs our marketing department. Smart as hell. Does great work, but she can't say 'No' to anyone. For example, all five of her direct staff wanted to go to a trade show. So, she let them ALL go, and she stayed back herself to mind the office when she should have gone to the show with a couple of them and left the other three behind."

"I see. Any other stories like that?"

"I have 50 more. Everyone loves her—her staff, colleagues . . . even me. But she's spreading herself too thin by trying to please everyone—especially me. She never stands up and says 'No.'"

J.C. laughed out loud and said, "Leo, I have to admit, I think you're the first CEO to ever complain to me about someone who always wants to do their bidding. Kudos to you!"

Leo chuckled on the other end and then asked, "Can you help?"

"I certainly will chat with her. Will she agree to that?"

"Are you kidding? If I asked her to walk across the Sahara Desert in her overcoat wearing ski pants, a hat, and gloves, she'd say yes!"

"Set it up, and we'll meet — not in the Sahara," J.C. said, smiling at the phone.

Chapter 4:
A Clearing in the Woods

J.C. had not taken on any partners, even though there was enough work. Instead, he had formed alliances with other coaches—two in particular, and both women—Allison Centarus and Elizabeth "Liz" Penrith whom he'd met at the UVa Hospital when he was ill. Allison had been a physician and Elizabeth had been a minister, but both by now had become master coaches and worked with very different clienteles and in their areas of professional expertise. Allison worked primarily with doctors, nurses, and healthcare executives; Elizabeth focused on ministers, boards of directors, and professional communicators. The three of them shared advice, laughter, and tears at their weekly meeting every Thursday. All their clients knew that they discussed their cases with one another and, in fact, had given their permission so that confidentiality would never be questioned.

On this particular Thursday at 4:00 p.m. J.C., Liz, and Allison met at J.C.'s office, where he had a fresh pot of brewed coffee ready. By now they had the ritual down. Allison was always on time and prepared with notes and a quick smile. This Thursday, Allison looked particularly exotic. In her mid-thirties, she had dark brown, shoulder-length curly hair, and wore tight, faded jeans, black leather boots, and a soft leather jacket from Nordstrom. When she entered the office, J.C. lost his concentration for a second or two. He got up to hug her and said, "Hey, great to see you."

She hugged him back and kissed him lightly on the cheek, which he willingly returned as he smelled her faint, elegant perfume. Then he remembered they were friends and broke free, a bit faster than she did.

"So where's Liz, or should I even ask?" Allison posed.

"How long have we been at this?"

"Point well taken."

About 10 minutes later, Liz bustled through the door, glitter sparkling in her hair. "Sorry, we just had Jeanie's birthday party . . . four years old. Can you believe that?" In her mid-forties, with auburn short cropped hair and blue eyes, Liz was tiny—a petite woman who looked more like she was a college sophomore than a successful executive coach and the mother of a four-year-old.

Allison just nodded and smiled at J.C., who laughed aloud, jumped up, and along with Allison, gave the harried mother-minister-coach a hug.

Soon they were sitting around a table talking about their clients. Allison went first.

"Jonathan, my neurosurgeon client, has hit a plateau. He doesn't feel like he's making progress."

"Tell us again about his issues."

"He's brilliant, and if I ever needed brain surgery, he'd be my surgeon. He also lacks the empathy gene . . . if you know what I mean."

Both J.C. and Liz nodded.

"Anyway, I asked him to read *Emotional Intelligence,* hoping it would help him understand better that he needs to develop that part of his brain. So, he did read it with a red pencil and pointed out to me every question he had with the book."

"But did he get the emotional intelligence stuff that applied to him?" J.C. asked.

"Yes and no. The guy is so smart and analytical that he has to dissect every thing or every person he encounters."

"How about a role play to help unfreeze his mindset?" Liz asked.

"Like what?"

J.C. joined in, "Like the movie *The Doctor* in which William Hurt played a doctor with cancer who had to go through all the waiting and humiliation that regular patients have to."

"Sure, I remember that movie. So, maybe ask him to pretend he's a patient in the hospital himself, with me acting like he does as the doctor—analytical and cool while the patient is an emotional wreck and falling apart."

"Yes," Liz said, "I've used that before with a lot of success with that bishop I once coached—you remember the guy who eventually became a writer?"

"Yeah, sure. I remember that. Kind of dramatic situation, as I recall," Allison said. "Yeah, I'll give that a try. Might just open him up to self-discovery. He's having difficulty with that right now, despite what the 360-degree evaluation revealed about him, in no uncertain terms."

"Sounds right from where I sit," J.C. said.

"Thanks, that helps me a lot. So, Liz, what about you?"

"My toughest client is me. I just can't seem to get organized or get ahead of the game. The hurrieder I go the behinder I get!"

"Have you tried keeping a weekly log that Allison suggested a few months ago?" J.C. asked.

"I did it for a day, then lost track of it on my desk and eventually forgot all about it," she said, shrugging her shoulders.

Allison looked at her and then at J.C. and roared.

"OK, have you ever thought about coupling your log writing to a daily ritual—connecting it to something you never forget to do?" J.C. asked, pausing for just a moment and then continuing, "What do you do each day without fail?"

Liz smiled. "I get up and take a shower every morning, then get breakfast for the family. Every night I take off my makeup, wash my face, and brush my teeth before going to bed."

"Perfect," J.C. said. "Keep your log in your bathroom and before you go to bed, write down everything you did that day. Be as specific as you can and include the time you spent doing those things."

"Great idea. And I'll try not to flush it down the toilet, like I did a few years ago with a small notebook that fell off the shelf over the toilet."

Her two friends laughed so hard they couldn't talk for a while.

Finally, J.C. said, "This time buy a larger notebook!" Then he and Allison burst out laughing again and Liz joined in.

"J.C., how about you?"

He then explained the second session he'd had with Stuart Samuelsson.

"He sounds like a hardball case," Allison said, "maybe we can get him and my neurosurgeon together as roommates."

Liz smiled and said, "I had a minister like him a year ago. Remember the guy the congregation wanted to toss out on his ear? He couldn't understand it at all. He'd pulled them from near bankruptcy to become a financially thriving church. Then they started losing members. Remember?"

"Yeah, wasn't he the guy who disliked visiting people in the hospital? Spent all his time with the accountant and the finance guys?"

"Bingo. He thought it was all about the bottom line. The guy should have been working on Wall Street, not at a church!"

"Maybe that's a clue to a possible path for my guy," J.C. said.

"Huh?" Liz said, "I was just joking."

"Yeah I know, but maybe Samuelsson would be better off on Wall Street . . . literally. I just never asked him."

"I'm a little lost here," Allison said.

"I see where J.C.'s going with this," Liz piped up.

"It's simple. If he calls me back—and that's a big if—I'm just going to ask him to design his perfect job, something he'd do for free if he had all the money in the world. The magic question."

"The magic question?" Allison asked.

"Yeah, I use it all the time with clients as a way of unfreezing their thinking. It goes like this: If something magical happened last night, and you no longer had to work for the money, but still had to work at something every day, what job would you do?"

"Perfect," Liz said, "I should have done that with my minister client. I know he would have said he'd have worked as a CPA!"

"Exactly," J.C. said, "And I'm predicting my guy will choose Wall Street."

The three of them chatted until Liz looked at the clock on the wall and jumped up. "I've got to pick up Jeanie in 15 minutes. Yikes!" And off she scooted, after pecking both J.C. and Allison on the cheek and running out the door.

"I'd better get going, too," Allison said.

Chapter 5:
One Tree at a Time

Sam Adams Sr. had founded III-Tech almost 15 years ago when he was 55 and newly retired from the federal government. He'd always wanted to have his own company, so the day he was eligible to leave Uncle Sam's employ, he took his money and ran. He tinkered around at several different projects for a while, until one day he saw his three-year-old grandson, Sam Adams III, playing with an electronic toy that spoke words and showed pictures. Sam III seemed mesmerized, repeating the words when he saw the pictures and before the speaker blurted out the answer. The faster Sam III hit the buttons, the quicker the images came up. A competitive child, Sam III relished speeding up the process.

But Sam Sr. began to think about the learning process and how he might want to design educational toys for kids like his grandson. So off he went with one of Sam III's old toys into his workshop. At first he merely took the game apart to see how it worked. Then he took out the microchips, had them scanned, read the code, and decided to create a few coded games of his own. At first it was basic stuff, but then he got more advanced.

Fast-forward 15 years. Sam III is about to go to college, his father Sam II has become a successful attorney who wants nothing to do with the tech company, and Sam Sr. wants to scale back his hours to be with his wife of 40 years. And while he has selected a potential internal candidate to take over as CEO, Sam Sr. is not 100 percent positive she will be the right fit. So, he calls J.C., who had been recommended to him through a colleague at a trade association for local high-tech companies called the

All-Technology Association, or ATA. Sam had been a member and a board officer of the association and was grateful for the referral to J.C.

"Well, Mr. Adams, it's nice to finally meet you after reading about you for so many years," J.C. said.

"Please, call me Sam — everybody else does. And thanks so much for coming by so quickly. I appreciate it."

"Of course. So, what's the issue that's bothering you?"

"I'm looking to step back from my business. I'm tired and would like to spend more time with my wife while we're both healthy enough to enjoy the great life we've built."

"I understand. And?"

"Well, I want the company and the 200 employees whose lives are affected by my decisions to be left in good hands."

"I see. Whose good hands?"

"Well, I used to think that would be my oldest boy, but he's a successful attorney and has no interest in the firm. His son, Sam III, for whom the company is named, in part, is just going off to college this fall."

"I see, so who's left?"

"Yes, well that's the issue. You see, Jane Smithfield has been the COO of the firm for the past five years. She's smart as the dickens . . . went to Stanford and MIT . . . a top-notch software engineer and an effective in-the-weeds kind of COO. Jane has her hands on the pulse, if not the throat, of the organization."

"Throat? Tell me more about why you used that word."

"Truth is, Jane can be a bit tenacious and independent. At times that's great, like when she's working on a very specific deliverable — get out of her way. But other times, her ferocious willpower can actually become suffocating. And she doesn't always tell everyone what's going on or what exactly she wants."

"I see. So, is she the likely prospect to replace you as CEO?"

"That's what I've been thinking, but I have strong reservations. The complaints I constantly hear from staff are that she's aloof and unapproachable and a steamroller."

J.C. laughs, "A steamroller! That's certainly descriptive. May I assume you mean that she's a my-way-or-the-highway kind of executive?"

"My way or you *become* the highway!" Sam chuckled back.

"I see."

Sam spoke again. "I believe the chief executive officer should be able to do many things well," he said. "Among them, she has to be a strategic, forward thinker, and a great networker inside and outside the company."

"I'd agree."

"Right now, Jane is lacking in both areas. Can you help?"

"Yes, I believe I can. But first I'd have to qualify her to be my client."

"Qualify her?"

"Yes. I don't accept clients who don't want to change. Executives get referred to me on a fairly frequent basis, but if they themselves don't see the need, they'll never change, and it's just a waste of time and money."

"I guess that makes sense. What else?"

"I never accept clients whose next step is being fired. I'll take clients with problems, but not someone who's one step away from termination."

"That's certainly not the case here. Jane's a very capable COO, and I would like nothing better than to promote her. And if she's not right for the CEO job, I hope she'll stay as the COO."

"I sensed that you thought pretty highly of her, but I wanted to give you a couple of concrete ways that I qualify clients. So, does she know you're bringing in someone to coach her?"

"Yes, we discussed it last week at lunch. She knows what her problems are, but I don't think she's aware of her effect on other people. At least I don't think she has a clear enough picture."

"I can help her with that. Typically, as part of my service, I conduct a 360-degree evaluation."

"A 360-degree evaluation?"

"Yes, I interview people, important stakeholder-type people, who are above, below, and at her own level. Sometimes that means reaching out to other COOs who know her as peers. I compile the information and discuss it with her. People are often surprised about how they're actually viewed by others. I won't say it's always a shock, but consistent themes will emerge and with a level of distinction and emotion that makes an indelible impression on the client."

"Like for instance?"

"She might define her style as honest and direct. But the feedback interviews with stakeholders—these are people whom she regards as important to her job and people she trusts—might say that she's insensitive and rude."

"Hmm, I see."

"So, when can I meet her to do my initial assessment—qualify her?"

"How about right now?"

Later, after Sam Sr. had made the introductions, he left J.C. with Jane in her spacious and sparse, almost cold, corner office.

"When do we begin?" she asked. Her piercing blue eyes seemed to bore a hole in J.C.

"Now, I suppose." He paused, looked out the window for a second, and then asked, "Why do you want to be the CEO?"

"Good question," she paused to think. "I suppose it's the next logical step."

"Logical step? Can you explain that?"

"I see life as a logically ordered process. This would be the next logical step for me."

"Has your life ever taken steps *not* in a logical sequence?"

"I don't believe so."

"No surprises, like death, a boyfriend breaking up with you, a friend moving away when you were a kid—something unexpected, even undeserved?"

"Well, of course. But I view them as accidents or anomalies."

"But did they change the course of your life?"

"Yes, I suppose so. That would be logical to assume."

J.C. smiled briefly and continued, "What's the single biggest challenge you think you would face as CEO?"

"All the schmoozing."

"Can you be specific?"

"Dealing with all the sensitive egos in the company, the board of advisors, our investors. I like dealing with the specific details of corporate execution, not with all the politics and drama."

"But dealing with all that would be part of the job as CEO. You do understand that?"

"Yes. And I accept that."

"But you'll be spending a lot of your time—most of your time—living in that world. I'm concerned that you might be taking this CEO job because you're expected to or it's 'the logical next step,' and not because you really want it."

For several seconds, she thought about what J.C. said. "I've had to work hard to learn what I did to get to where I am now," she said. "I'm willing to work hard again to lead this company. I think we can go places, and I'm willing to step up to make that happen."

"OK. How much do you know about executive coaching?"

"Several of my friends have coaches and have explained the process to me. And ever since Sam raised the issue, I've been reading a lot about it on the Web."

"So, you understand that I ask more questions than I answer?"

"I gathered that, yes."

"I'm not an expert in the specifics of what you do."

"I realize that."

"So, how do you think coaching could help you?"

"First, Sam thinks it's a good idea, and I have a lot of respect for him. Second, this isn't the first time I've had leadership issues. I thought it was about time for me to deal with them—head on—not only for the future of the company but also for myself."

"Good, because I think together we can make that happen. So pull out your calendar, and let's set up a couple meetings a month for the next three months and roll up our sleeves to start working hard."

She smiled briefly and turned to her PDA to find open dates.

Chapter 6:
Autumn Leaves Fall

Stuart Samuelsson's assistant, Marie Collingwood, called J.C. on his cell phone and said, "Mr. Williams, I'm afraid that Mr. Samuelsson is not doing very well."

"I'm sorry to hear that, Marie. What's wrong?"

"He's . . ." she hesitated, "I think, he's under a lot of stress."

"About what?"

"I really shouldn't even be calling you. I just didn't know what to do to help him. He's a decent man. . . ." her voice trailed off.

"Is he physically sick?"

"Not exactly." She paused to think. "His wife left him and the business is going badly, and . . . well, he's drinking quite a bit."

"I'm sorry for him and for you. How can I help you?"

"Someone needs to talk to him."

"I can do that if you'd like, but I'm not sure he wants to see me."

"I can arrange it if I say you insisted on seeing him. I know he respects you—he has said several positive things about you. Let me try to set up a meeting, if that's OK with you."

"Sounds good. Just let me know."

"Thank you, sir," she said and hung up.

The next week at 9:00 a.m., almost a full month since their last meeting, J.C. walked into Stuart Samuelsson's large office. The office was in disarray, with charts, graphs, and stacks of folders containing financial and marketing data strewn across the floor.

J.C. navigated the clutter to get to Stuart, who was sitting in his large leather chair in one corner of the office. His tie was pulled down, his shirt open and somewhat wrinkled, and sleeves rolled. He was chewing a breath mint.

"Stuart, how's it going?"

Stuart looked around his battlefield of an office. His next words were slightly slurred. "How's it look like I'm doing?"

"OK, how are you feeling?"

"Like I need anoth . . . Like I need a drink."

"Have you been drinking today?"

"What are you, the sobriety cop?"

"No, of course not, just concerned."

"Well what do you want?"

"Just checking in. How's your family?"

"None of your business. Now what the hell do you want? I'm a busy guy trying to run a business that's in the tank. So, what is it?"

"May I make an observation?"

"Here we go again with the mother-may-I bullshit. Speak your mind, man. I've got work to do."

"OK. First, your office has deteriorated considerably since I was last here only a month ago. Sometimes that's a sign. Second, you don't look good—your eyes are bloodshot, you look exhausted, and you don't appear to be getting any energy from your job. Finally, you're chewing breath mints and talking about drinking at 9:00 in the morning."

"Thanks, Sigmund Freud. So what's your diagnosis?"

"Because you asked, I'll be frank. I think you are losing your grip, have turned to alcohol to self-medicate, and are slipping deeper into a hole that's becoming increasingly more difficult to climb out of. I think you need to see a therapist and quickly. You need to talk to somebody, now."

"Bullshit. Therapists are nuts trying to find themselves in their patients. Besides I can just hire you to talk to," he said, pulling out his checkbook and pen. "What's your monthly retainer, kid?"

J.C. didn't answer for a few moments. Then he said slowly and deliberately, "Please put away your checkbook. You can't hire me now."

"Yes, I can. Got plenty of budget left."

"That's not what I mean. I won't, I can't work for you. Ethically, I have to refer you to a healthcare specialist—someone more qualified than I to help you with your current problem."

"Current problem?"

Staring at him directly, J.C. said, "I think you have a serious drinking problem that can lead to more issues, like depression."

"Bullshit."

J.C. breathed deeply and collected himself. He hated this kind of intervention, but had done more than his share in his practice. In fact, in his first year when revenues were thin and the expense file was plenty thick with all manner of start-up costs, he actually turned down more revenue than he billed because of just such problems—clients who came to him from worried chairmen, senior staffers, even wives and husbands. He'd sworn to stand on his ethical two legs and not take clients who would otherwise be better served by medical, spiritual, or mental health professionals. "Executive coaching works with the worried well, not folks who have an illness or are in deep need of a personal counselor," one of J.C.'s professors at Darden had told him once.

"Get the hell out of here. Now!" Stuart bellowed.

Trying not to trip on the debris on the floor, J.C. walked calmly toward the door. When he reached it, he turned and said, "Stuart, I wish you good luck. Please consider seeing someone soon."

Stuart didn't even bother to look up.

On his way out, J.C. stopped at Marie's desk.

"Marie, I can't discuss much with you, but I'm giving you the name of a good doctor who might be able to help if Stuart ever agrees to see one, which frankly I'm not at all sure he will."

"Thank you so much, Mr. Williams."

"It's J.C., not Mr. Williams. And good luck."

She nodded and forced a faint smile.

Two days later at 10:00 p.m., Marie called J.C. Her voice was rapid and higher pitched than before. "Stuart's . . . I mean Mr. Samuelsson's had a heart attack I think. He's," she paused, "at my apartment. I tried to call 911 but he yelled at me not to. He's in the bathroom on the floor and looks awful. What should I do?"

"What's your address?"

"I'm at the Berkshire Apartments at 1201 Courthouse, Apartment 103. Are you coming over soon?"

"No, I'll meet you at the hospital. I'm calling 911 right now."

"Thank you."

An hour later J.C. arrived at the emergency room waiting area and found Marie looking like she'd been up all night crying.

"How is he?"

"The doctor won't tell me anything. I'm not his family," she said, wringing her hands. "But the nurse has been very nice. He said everything looks fine. He said that Stuart . . ." She started to correct herself but saw how futile that was now that J.C. had already surmised they were having an affair. "Stuart has angina, chest pains, but it doesn't look like there's any heart damage, thank God. Stress is what the nurse told me the doctor wrote down."

"Not a big surprise at all."

"No."

At 3:15 a.m., the orderly pushed Stuart out to the nearly deserted waiting room. Marie had dozed off, but J.C. was still awake, barely. He roused Marie, who bolted upright, saw Stuart, and rushed to his side. "Stuart, I was so worried. How are you?"

Samuelsson looked as if he'd aged ten years from the last time J.C. had seen him. Gaunt, pasty white, and with at least two days' beard stubble on his face, he appeared only a few degrees shy of being unkempt. When Marie turned to grab her coat and search for her car keys, Samuelsson saw J.C. and just shook his head. He was disgusted at having been seen in his current condition.

J.C. asked Marie if she needed any help getting Stuart back home.

"No, but thank you. I really appreciate your coming down. I'm, I didn't know what to do. He was so . . ."

"No problem. I'll see you later."

And without saying a word, he walked by Stuart, whose head was slumped down as he stared at the floor. J.C. patted him on the shoulder and then headed back to his car.

Chapter 7:
A Clearing in the Forest

J.C. had met with Ann Tabor, the too-nice marketing executive, and they'd hit it off immediately. And as Leo had promised, J.C. had instant affection for his new client. Their first two meetings had gone well, with deep discussions about Ann's personality, her place in life, and her difficulty with saying "no" and confronting people, especially direct reports.

The next two weeks were both enlightening and challenging for Ann. She had to do her job—strategically leading her company's marketing efforts. At the same time, she did the homework that J.C. had given her to help meet her challenges. She was keeping up by working for a few hours every weekend.

But her real challenge came when she had to put her homework into practice. That challenge came on the day she had to tell one of her key employees, Brad Sampson, that he would not head up the marketing team for the new brand that their company would launch. She and J.C. had actually practiced the tough conversation together in role play: one time Ann acted out Brad's part, and in another round, she played herself while J.C. acted like Brad. So she got to see the scenario from both perspectives, which J.C. explained was the way to approach tough conversations— from the recipient's point of view first, then your own.

Finally, the day came, and Brad Sampson sat in her office. He was all smiles—thinking that good news was coming his way.

"Brad, I know how hard you've worked this past year, and I appreciate what you've accomplished. I really do. And, I had to make a decision about who should take the lead on the new branding effort. I considered you—long and hard—and ultimately decided on giving the lead to Sam. I—"

Brad quickly interrupted her. "What?" A cloud appeared to reform his face.

"I have assigned the lead to Sam."

"To Sam? Why?"

"I'm guessing you're upset. I know I would be. Especially, given all you've done—how hard you've worked."

"Damned right! Frankly, I'm stunned."

"I understand that completely, and I want to explain my reasoning to—"

He interrupted her again. "I'm too angry to talk right now, Ann," he said, then rose and walked out.

Ann remained silent and called J.C. after the door slammed shut. Clearly upset over the incident, she told J.C. it had gone terribly and, at J.C.'s request, recounted the conversation nearly verbatim.

"So why did you think it went badly?"

"I hurt his feelings. He stormed out on me."

"Listen, he's absorbing difficult information. It will take some time, but eventually he'll come to grips with it. Tough conversations are tough because they're not easy."

"Now that sounds like breakthrough research!"

J.C. laughed. "Look, you approached the conversation recognizing how he must feel, so he knows you're empathetic. That's huge in having a tough conversation—starting from his perspective, not your own. But being understanding and empathetic doesn't mean giving into a bad choice."

"Yes, but he feels terrible. And so do I."

"It's going to take time for him to accept this whole thing. He's actually going to go through the grief process.

You know what it's like to lose out on something you've wanted, right? At first you don't believe it, you're in denial—then you're really mad. You even think you can probably argue or bargain your way into getting what you want. Sometimes, as a defense, you even tell yourself you don't care . . . until it finally sinks in and you're ready to accept it and move on."

"That sounds like what I'm feeling—denial—that I actually did that to him."

"That makes sense because you've just lost your comfortable relationship with this guy, and you're starting to grieve that loss too. Give it time."

"I guess."

"Trust me, you've done well!"

"I don't feel like it."

"Hey, if this leadership thing were easy, anyone could do it."

Chapter 8:
A Tall Tree in the Forest

David Blackmon was an imposing man. Tall, blond, athletic, and good looking, he had been the quarterback on his college football team 15 years ago and the class president. At 6'5" he towered like a sequoia over most everyone he met, and when he strutted into a room, women noticed and men got just a bit more edgy. It would be safe to call David an alpha male.

J.C. first met him socially at a large community foundation, where David was the executive director and CEO. They exchanged niceties and business cards, but neither of them followed up on the connection until J.C. got a call from the chairperson of the foundation, Max Ingersoll. After an introduction including the reference to one of J.C.'s former clients, Max said quite candidly, "I'm more than a bit concerned about David's relationship with the board." J.C. remained quiet to ensure that Max did most of the talking. Like J.C.'s dad, Walt, used to say, "You can't actively fish unless you're willing to wait."

Max continued, "David's a bit curt, if not at times dismissive, even disrespectful."

"How so?"

"At the last board meeting, one of the board members questioned David's conduct at the last event the foundation put on in May. David was supposed to introduce me as the chairperson and then step aside, while I was to introduce the speaker. Instead, David introduced me and then introduced the speaker, so I had to sit down and was placed in a very awkward position. We had words after the dinner, but David brushed it off saying that it just worked better that way and was no big deal."

"And did it disrupt the proceedings?"

"Not really. But his uncaring rudeness was just an example of the attitude he displays to everyone. It's like he's in a movie, and he has to be the star; everyone else is a supporting actor."

"I see. And the effect on the organization?"

"Hard to measure just yet. But I've asked the accountant to look at every dime coming in and going out."

"Why? Do you expect foul play?"

"Just making sure. The impact, you know. I'm a numbers man."

"Well, what would you like me to do?"

"I thought we'd give this coaching thing a whirl and see."

"A whirl? Can you tell me what you mean by that?"

"I have a good friend who's a consultant—a very successful one. He's a man I trust, and he advised me to look into executive coaching for David. I called another friend and former client of yours, so here I am. I'm willing to give it a try."

After they talked for a while longer, J.C. explained that he never accepted an assignment without talking to the client first. "Would David be willing?" J.C. asked.

"Truthfully, I don't know. He has a rather large ego."

"Well, the good news is that most CEOs have strong personalities; it's almost required for the job. So, to broach the subject of coaching, you might want to present it as a perk rather than penance."

"How so?"

"Many of my clients consider executive coaching as professional leadership development. Sort of getting help one-on-one. It is intense and personally tailored, and has definite outcomes, most of which directly affect the life of the CEO and the future of the company."

After a bit more discussion, Max agreed that David would like that approach. So, J.C. agreed to a lunch with David if Max would set it up.

Two weeks later, J.C. arrived at the French restaurant to find that David was not there yet, so he settled himself on a chair in the foyer and began reading a magazine that he pulled from a rack near the hosting station. He thumbed through, found a long article on what makes CEOs tick, and began to read it with great interest. About 15 minutes later, he looked up and still no David, so he dipped his head down again and read another piece. After nearly half an hour had passed, David sauntered in and said, "Hello, I'm David Blackmon. You must be J.C."

"Yes, hello David, we met last year at your gala in May."

He looked at J.C. then turned to the host and said, "David Blackmon for two."

They were seated near the bay window at one of David's favorite tables. Evidently he was well known there, judging by the way the staff fell all over him. After the waiter laid a linen napkin in both their laps—David's first, then his guest's—J.C. looked at him and asked, "Did you get held up in traffic?"

"No. In fact, I got here quickly."

"Not from where I was sitting."

"I took a call from a friend just before I left."

"Not one you could have returned later?"

There was no response. David was deeply into reading his menu, almost completely ignoring J.C.

"David," he said, "David," J.C. said a second time, more loudly.

And when David lifted his head with an annoyed look, J.C. said, "I don't think this will work." And with that he stood up and walked out of the restaurant, leaving behind the bewildered golden boy to dine solo and contemplate what had just happened.

When J.C. returned to his office, he e-mailed Max to follow up. Max's reply was short but telling: "Good for you."

The next day J.C. got an e-mail from David that simply said, "The friend I took the call from had been very ill for a long time. I thought it was more important to talk to him. Let's try lunch again, shall we?"

J.C.'s note back: "OK."

This time David showed up five minutes early at the same restaurant. They were seated and eating when David said, "Look, Max wants me to go to charm school with you."

"Charm school?"

"Hey, I'm well aware that Max and I, and now a few board members, don't always see eye-to-eye. Boards are like that. You're trying to balance some pretty big egos."

"What's a big ego look like?"

"Guys who have only one point of view, theirs."

"Anything else?"

"They usually have a strong need to be the center of attention, that sort of stuff."

"What else?"

"They can be disrespectful of my time."

"Like being late for meetings?" J.C. said as he put his fork down and stared directly at David.

David blinked. "Touché."

J.C. nodded slightly.

Chapter 9:
A Storm Blows Through

A couple of weeks later, J.C.'s office phone rang at 7:19 p.m. It was his strategic partner and colleague, Allison Centarus. When he heard the high pitch of her voice, J.C. knew that it was important. "J.C., I need to see you tonight. Liz is out of town, but I've got to talk to you today."

"Hey, you sound upset."

"Goddamned right."

This was the worst word he'd ever heard the normally objective, former physician utter.

"I'm being sued by a coaching client!"

"Oh my. How soon can you come by?"

"I'm on my way."

By 8:00, Allison had arrived and was sitting in J.C.'s office, having been offered, and accepted, a glass of Chardonnay. In the first 10 minutes, she explained the situation: Since Allison had left the hospital to become an executive coach, the hospital's CEO had regularly sent her some good clients. One day he'd asked her to meet him. It was urgent—one of the physicians on staff, a brilliant neurosurgeon, had been sued for the third time this year, and the Board of Directors was going nuts over all the lawsuits and liability exposure. They had wanted to terminate the physician's services summarily, but the CEO did not. The surgeon was the best on the East Coast, he argued, and his family had given incredible amounts of money to the hospital's foundation. So, the CEO convinced them to bring in an executive coach—one who herself was an MD. The board loved the idea, and Allison took the assignment to help bail out the CEO.

Her first meeting with the surgeon, Jonathan Jeffries, had made Allison wish she had not violated her own first rule of coaching—always qualify the client for fit. She'd learned from experience to trust her gut when it came to determining the coachable and the uncoachable. And all kinds of red flags went up the first time she met Jonathan Jeffries. He was arrogant, dogmatic, and uncompromising. He thought the board's idea that he receive mandatory executive coaching was preposterous. He repeatedly questioned Allison's impeccable qualifications.

Yet Allison had worked with him once a week for six months. It had been torture. He was repeatedly late or cancelled. He had refused to set down any goals or objectives that in any way looked conciliatory to the board. And, he fought her and the board like a petulant child. For example, in the monthly updates the board required— which involved three-way meetings between the board, Jeffries, and Allison to assess Jeffries' progress—he was recalcitrant, obstinate, and uncooperative, debating every single issue. Finally, they tired of his antics and fired him.

That's when he promptly sued the board and Allison. The board was covered by corporate counsel and Board of Directors' insurance, but Allison soon found out that she was on her own, and Jeffries had a pile of money and a cousin known to be a great white shark among the legal ranks.

"This jerk could bankrupt me by dragging out this frivolous lawsuit," she said, taking a larger-than-normal gulp of the wine.

"OK. I'd say that's worst-case scenario. So what's best case?"

"He drops the suit, and I sue him for defamation!"

"Let's stick with he drops the suit, shall we? So, what might make him drop the suit?"

"A miracle."

"OK, what could that miracle look like?"

"Hey, are you coaching me now?"

"It's what we do for our clients, isn't it?"

"OK. I'll play along. Best-case scenario is he gets hit by a bus!"

J.C. almost chokes on his wine, then regains his composure. "Come on."

"Well, I guess the hospital could put on enough pressure to make him pay attention. They could report all his antics to the State Medical Board—build a case against his license. That might get his attention."

"That's one approach. Any others?" J.C. asked, sitting back in his chair.

"I could convince the board to roll me into their suit as a former colleague and still-licensed physician. I didn't give up my privileges when I resigned."

"Good thought," he said. "And?" he asked, prompting her.

As Allison sipped her wine and mused, J.C. asked, "Is there anyone whom he respects—anyone who influences his decisions?"

"His father, the old man. Ronald Jeffries was quite a businessman and set up Jonathan for his whole life."

"What's he do now?" J.C. asked.

"Retired, living on the beach in Delaware—Rehoboth Beach, I think," Allison said.

"Really. My family has vacationed there for more than 30 years. Interesting. What kind of guy is he?" J.C. was leaning forward now, intrigued.

"Supposed to be a great guy."

"So could he be another avenue?"

"I never would have thought so, but now that you mention it, sure. He's definitely worth considering."

"Any more thoughts?"

She rolled her eyes back and forth as if she were trying to picture, think, or hear something they could use for the exercise. "Nope, but you got me thinking. I'll work on it the rest of this week and pull together a list."

"This is a great start. I want to see you in a week with the following in hand. First, I want you write out as many positive resolutions as you can. Add to the three we brainstormed today. Then research them and come up with several concrete tactical principles. When you come back next week, we'll go through them, prioritize them, and get started ticking them off your list. How's that sound?"

"Like a plan. Wonderful," she said as she stood up and hugged him. "Thanks, J.C.," she said and gave him a kiss on his cheek—the second kiss this month, he thought to himself. And he held her for an extra second or two, for his benefit, not hers.

After she left his office, he did some research about Jonathan Jeffries and especially about his father, Ronald Jeffries. Turns out that Ronald Jeffries had also started out as a solo consultant. He'd been active in the community and a generous man. But most importantly, he'd been a big basketball fan of George Mason University, as was J.C., who further noted that Ronald lived on the North Shore of Rehoboth Beach in the posh community of Henlopen Acres—an area where J.C. had vacationed with his family since he was a kid.

That's when he thought a trip to his old vacation stomping ground might be in short order. J.C. knew he would enjoy the trip, but would have to get permission from Allison first.

Chapter 10:
In the Saw Grass

Allison had been not only supportive of J.C.'s idea about visiting Ronald Jeffries, she'd also volunteered to accompany him to Rehoboth. They booked two hotel rooms and began investigating.

According to intelligence that J.C. was able to get from some neighbors in Henlopen Acres, Ronald fished in the surf every morning just north of the Henlopen condos, and he was a creature of strong habit. On the trip up from Virginia, J.C. and Allison had brainstormed a number of approaches. One scenario involved J.C. inviting Ronald and a mutual friend to dinner—someone from the Acres. J.C. also thought about sending an e-mail ahead of time. But after mulling over the options, he decided to just walk up to Ronald, explain the situation, and see how he handled it.

After getting Allison settled in her room, J.C. visited a close friend of the family, Archie Tenucci. Tenucci was a neighbor in Henlopen Acres with whom J.C.'s family had become close over the years, especially after J.C.'s mother had helped Archie the summer his wife died. J.C.'s mother had pulled him through with visits, phone calls, cards, and letters. J.C.'s parents even had Archie stay at their house in McLean for a week over Christmas that year.

"Archie, how the heck are you?" J.C. said as he pulled the tall, overweight former college football star to himself.

"J.C., how the hell are you, boy?" Archie said, enveloping the smaller, much thinner man in a bear hug.

Within minutes the two were in Archie's den laughing about all the summers, the girls, the antics that accumulated over the years when J.C. and his family, friends, and relatives invaded the tiny quiet hamlet of

Henlopen Acres for the summer. "You remember that Fourth of July when you and your brilliant buddies launched that rocket and damned near took out that police car on patrol? That officer was one pissed-off fellow," Archie said, laughing and slapping J.C. on the back so hard it could have been used on a choking person as a Heimlich maneuver.

"Sure do. And thanks for bringing it up again," he said rolling his eyes. "I don't think I've ever seen my father so mad."

"Yep, Big Walt was steamed."

J.C. and Archie talked for a few more minutes when J.C. turned the conversation toward Jonathan and Ronald Jeffries. He explained the lawsuit, Allison, and his plan to talk to Ronald, and asked how well Archie knew his neighbor from down the street.

"Ron's a great guy. That's the long and short of it. I never did like that kid of his, Jonathan. That kid was a pain in everyone's behind for years."

"Well, it appears he's remained consistent. And, his lawsuit could bankrupt my friend Allison; it's just unfair and mean spirited. So, I'd like to talk to Ronald Jeffries tomorrow to see if this litigation can be stopped. I understand that he fishes every day at the end of the boardwalk near the Henlopen Hotel."

"Yep, every day with a thermos of coffee. Set your watch by him — 6:00 to 8:00 — and then he gets breakfast at the Henlopen."

"I'm thinking of just going up to him and talking to him straight. What do you think?"

"He's a plain-spoken man. Don't think he'd take offense. Just let him get a couple of cups of coffee in him first. Maybe walk by at 7:00 or so. Besides, even he thinks his own kid's a jerk. But, he's still Jonathan's daddy. Remember that."

"Good information, Archie, and a great point."

That night J.C. had a wonderful dinner with Allison, who had spent the day writing a paper to present at an upcoming International Coaching Federation conference, in between worrying about her lawsuit. As they ate, J.C. told her of his afternoon with Archie. He explained all the relationships and told her that he'd be meeting with Ronald Jeffries early the next morning on the beach. They went back to his room, talked a while longer, drank some wine— and then she went to her room, but not after a warm "goodnight" embrace, which kept J.C. thinking about well after she had left.

The next morning was foggy and cool, so J.C. threw on his sweatshirt and running pants and at 6:45 headed out the door for a run to the beach. As he passed down Rehoboth Avenue, he looked at all the restaurants and stores he and his family had frequented during their wonderful summers. Browseabout Books reminded him of the endless hours he'd spent with his buddies, reading and stalking the aisles for new books, magazines, and girls, anything to pass time, get out of the sun, or spend a rainy afternoon. The place had become an icon of Rehoboth Beach and had inspired J.C. to become an avid reader. He had gone to so many lectures by visiting writers, they were hard to recall, except that many times, J.C. was the youngest male there. In a number of author talks, he was the only male present, especially when women romance authors spoke. But J.C. could not get enough of hearing about authors and how, what, and why they wrote. All this had inspired him to write as well. It was at Rehoboth that he started to keep a journal, and it was his journal that kept him sane when he'd fought cancer.

When he hit the boardwalk, J.C. encountered more runners and an occasional bike rider—nothing like the kind of crowd that mobbed the stretch of boardwalk during the summers. He ran past Dolly's Saltwater Taffy, past the Atlantic Sands, the Boardwalk Plaza Hotel, One Virginia Avenue, and finally past the Henlopen, where he stopped to take off his running shoes and socks and walk to the water.

When he crossed the jetty, just north of the hotel, he spotted a solitary figure standing next to a long, sea-fishing pole being held in the ground by a two-foot tall plastic stand. The pole's fishing line soared well above the sand, which later would be filled with kids and sunbathers, and extended to the sea in search of fish. Ronald Jeffries was a tall, though now somewhat slumped, man in his early eighties. He wore a yellow and blue nylon windbreaker and a green and gold George Mason University baseball hat.

To cool down his legs, J.C. walked up to his knees in the surf well south of where Ronald was fishing. There were a handful of other early morning beach walkers out, so Ronald didn't even seem to register J.C.'s presence. After a few minutes, J.C. made his way up the beach and then turned from the wet-packed sand toward Ronald Jeffries, who while still sipping his coffee, picked up the young sweaty jogger on his cautionary radar.

"Hello. Are you Mr. Jeffries?"

Looking more than skeptical, Jeffries, said, "Yes, I am."

"I'm J.C. Williams, sir. My family has summered in Henlopen Acres for 30 years. Walt Williams was my dad."

Jeffries paused to absorb the information and then responded, "Walt was a good man. Sorry to hear about his passing away."

"Thanks, we all miss him very much."

"So what brings you to the beach in October?"

"To be straightforward, sir, you."

"Me?"

"Well, indirectly. Your son, Jonathan, is suing his old hospital and my friend who had been trying to coach him."

At that Ronald shook his head and looked down at the sand but said nothing.

So, J.C. continued. "My friend, Allison, is a medical doctor and an executive coach. She's highly regarded by everyone and has never done a mean thing to anyone in her life. Now she'll be dragged through a court system, will need to hire a lawyer, and may go out of business because of lawyers' fees over this whole mess."

"So, why are you talking to me?"

"Frankly, because I'm hoping you can change Jonathan's mind."

"That kid . . ." Ronald stopped short of saying any more.

"Well, I thought he might at least listen to you."

Ronald looked out at the sea and thought for some time. "A long time ago, your dad, Walt, helped me solve a nasty business problem with a *Washington Post* reporter who just would not get off my butt about a land purchase I'd made," he said. "That reporter was certain that I was doing something illegal—which I was not. One day, on just about this same spot on the beach, Walt offered to call him up for me and straighten him out. Walt did what he promised, and the kid just went away. I never forgot that."

Surprised, even stunned that he'd never heard about Walt giving help to such a successful businessman, J.C. just said, "Dad was a great guy."

"He was, son. And I have a theory that acorns don't fall too far from the tree. So, I'm going to help your friend on one condition."

"Yes sir, what's that?"

"Actually two conditions as I think of it. First, you never mention to my son that we talked."

"Of course. And the second?"

"That you tell your mother how much I think of your father and how sorry I was not to have made it to the funeral. I was out of the country."

"Done, Mr. Jeffries."

"Tell your friend this lawsuit will go away. Trust me," he said as he looked J.C. in the eye, never blinking until he turned his head back toward the sea.

"Yes, sir."

Later that morning when he and Allison were eating breakfast, J.C. told her about his run, the surf, and his chat with Ronald Jeffries. He took his time giving her details. He could feel her edging forward in her seat, breathing faster, her eyes unblinking. He explained the fog, the cool surf, the smooth sand, the sun breaking through the fog, the solitary figure of Mr. Jeffries. With each detail, Allison seemed more anxious for the climax of the story.

But J.C. was not letting her off so quickly. Detail after detail, sights, sounds, smells, and words teased out of his lips. He told her the story about how Walt had helped Mr. Jeffries, about how much Ronald thought of Walt. Allison was nearly wild by this point. "So what did he say about the lawsuit, please tell me, please!"

"He looked down at me with a stare . . ." J.C.'s voice trailed off as he paused to sip his wine. Meanwhile, Allison had moved so close to the edge of her chair that it was tipping forward.

"Will you please tell me what he said!"

"He looked me straight in the eye and said . . ."—J.C. slowed down to say the next sentence with clarity and simplicity—". . . 'Tell your friend this lawsuit will go away. Trust me.'"

With that Allison threw up her hands and screamed, "Yes, yes, yes!" Then she slammed the table and reached across it to give J.C. a passionate kiss, which he returned with equal passion.

Chapter 11:
Back in the Bushes

The first appointment J.C. had after he returned from Rehoboth was with Jane Smithfield—the top-notch software engineer and COO who had her hands on the pulse, if not the throat, of III-Tech, as Sam Adams had put it. When J.C. entered her corner office, he noticed how sterile it was—virtually nothing on the walls except her Stanford and MIT diplomas on a side wall, barely visible. She had a few pictures of family—parents, children, and what looked like grandparents—all in small frames on her credenza. Her desk had been cleared of any clutter. The place could have been a clinical examination room in a hospital, J.C. thought, as Jane motioned him to sit in the straight-backed chair that faced her desk.

J.C. looked around and found a couch and chair in the corner—probably a leftover from a previous tenant—and said, "How about over here? It will be more comfortable and efficient for what we'll be doing." The word efficient must have struck a reflexive chord, because after a moment's thought, she got up and followed his pointing finger toward the conversation nook and took her seat in the large, single chair. Interesting, J.C. thought.

After they'd been seated, he said, "Well, how's it going?"

"Fine," she said. He waited, but she remained silent.

"OK, let's get started. The first phase of this six-month engagement will be self-discovery."

"Self-discovery," she said, "I already know who I am. This seems like a distraction."

"I know it might seem that way now, but it will be the basis for making decisions along the way—it's important." She raised her eyebrows as if to say, "Whatever."

Over the next hour, J.C. discussed their agreement. He told her about confidentiality—he would not tell anyone about their relationship nor discuss progress with human resources or the CEO unless she gave her explicit permission. In fact, he preferred that she, not he, give any updates to management. He talked about what he called the adaptation cycle, and how their relationship would have its ups and downs over the next six months, but that they'd work through them. They discussed the best dates and times to meet, the nature of goal setting and assignments, the keeping of notes on their progress, and a host of other administrative details that he always covered in the initial meeting to set expectations and eliminate any vagueness about the process. When he mentioned defining her nagging inner voices, she looked very puzzled and said, "What did you say?"

"Those are the voices hiding deep inside us that want to maintain the status quo. The inner voice wants things to stay just the way they are. Otherwise, you have to adapt your thinking—do some work," he explained. "In a larger context, prejudice and bias are the result of a nagging inner voice. It's easier for people to discount others who are different. In one way, it simplifies life for them—they don't have to deal with that segment of the population. Of course, doing that maintains the status quo but makes incredible errors of omission. On a work-a-day basis, procrastination might be the by-product of an inner voice. Not attacking a problem but putting it off until another day keeps things in play and maintains the status quo. We all have them. We'll want to define your inner voice so that we can identify it when it comes up and keeps you from making changes."

"I don't have any. I'm fine."

"Well, there's one already."

"What?"

"The 'I'm fine' inner voice. That one keeps things untouchable, shuts down communication, and maintains the status quo," he said, making a note.

"Whatever."

"OK, so we have two: 'I'm fine' and 'whatever.'"

She just sat there, nearly fuming under her breath. J.C. wanted to add a third, "The Silent Treatment," but decided not to push her too hard the first meeting. After an hour had passed, he told her that they'd meet face to face twice a month for an hour and a half, and she agreed. Then he said, "I need to give you several assignments for next week."

"Assignments?"

"Let's call it field work, but yes, you need to get them done for us to proceed."

"Whatever," she said.

"There's your inner voice talking."

She just shrugged.

"I'll need you to pick a single priority that you'd like to work on for the next few weeks. It should be business related. Think about one observable behavior that, were you able to change it, would make a big difference in your performance. You may want to choose something that's come up in performance appraisal conversations in the past."

She took notes but did not respond.

"Also, I will need a list of 360 stakeholders."

She gave him a quizzical look.

"Let me explain. I'll use the CEO, your boss, but I'll also need the names of three people below you—directors or VPs—and three people at your level—colleagues or peers, like other COOs in other companies. These must be people whom you trust and whose opinions you respect. I'll need this in two days to get started on your 360 Continue-Stop-Start."

This time she looked at him in complete confusion. "Continue, stop, start?"

"Sorry. Yes. I ask people who serve in the organization above, below, and at the same level as you to tell me what you're doing well and should *continue* to do to advance, what you need to *stop* doing to stop hurting yourself, and what you should *start* doing to do an even better job."

"Wait, explain 'hurting myself.'"

"We all do things, often unconsciously, that hurt our cause. For example, the executive who badgers people in staff meetings might not be aware of what he's doing to shut down discussion, let alone destroy employee morale and confidence. This process unearths that kind of thing."

"And they tell you this stuff?"

"Absolutely. First, I require that you have to tell them that I'll be interviewing them and that you really want them to be candid. Then, they have to trust that I'll keep their comments confidential."

"And how do you do that?"

"I aggregate their comments into clusters, trends. I also make sure that I eliminate any references that might signal who said what. Then I give you an oral report so that you don't try to dissect and over-analyze the results. Some clients try very hard to determine who said what about them. That's a destructive activity, when the purpose is to discover strengths and challenges."

"I guess."

"Believe me, it works. I also need you to read a few articles I'm going to leave with you that explain the nature of coaching. And finally, I'd like you to start keeping a coaching journal. You can write anything you want. For example, after I leave you can write your initial impressions," he said and smiled. She did not smile back. "The journal will help you a lot with your reports to me."

"Reports?"

"Yes, every time before we meet, I'll need you to e-mail me a report, a short summary, of what you've done or read, your reactions, your movement toward the goals—that sort of thing."

"What goals?"

"That comes soon. Let's not get ahead of ourselves. For now, let's stay in the discovery phase. By the way, I'd like to get your Myers-Briggs type if you know that. And, I'd like you to take an instrument I'll leave with you to help me know what your strengths are. It's based on a book you'll need to buy called *Now, Discover Your Strengths,* and you take the Strength Finder instrument online. I think that's enough for next time."

"I'd say," she said as J.C. got to his feet, shook her hand, and excused himself. When he got to the door, he turned and said, "Oh by the way, I'll need your report 48 hours before we meet."

She started to mouth the word *whatever,* when J.C. pointed and began to mouth the words *nagging inner voice.* She checked herself, looked at him, and turned toward her desk.

He turned away from her toward the door and smiled to himself.

Chapter 12:
On the Path

J.C. had just returned from his morning run when the phone in his office began to ring. While he was tempted to let it go to voice mail, he saw the readout on his cell phone: Samuelsson Technology. *Stuart Samuelsson,* J.C. thought to himself, *this should be interesting.*

The voice on the other end of the phone belonged to Stuart's assistant. "J.C., this is Marie Collingwood. Are you available to talk with Stuart, I mean Mr. Samuelsson?"

"Sure, but after I take a shower. I just got back from a run. Does he want to talk over the phone or in person and when?"

"I think he'd rather do it in person. Can you come by sometime today?"

J.C. flipped through his PDA and said, "Sure, let's say this afternoon, about 2:00."

That day, J.C. reviewed his notes on Stuart just to make sure he hadn't missed anything before going in for the interview. But he knew the meeting might be awkward at first—more for Samuelsson than himself. The key, he thought, was to try to put himself in his potential client's shoes—remain empathetic—despite Samuelsson's overbearing, irascible personality.

When Marie ushered J.C. into Stuart's office, J.C. knew right away that things had changed. The office was clean, neat, and devoid of stacks of paper, coffee cups, or cigarettes. Even Samuelsson looked very different—less rumpled, more crisp, and most notably, the guy actually smiled as he rose to get up and come from around his desk to greet J.C.

"J.C., good to see you."

"Stuart, you're looking well."

"Trying hard."

"That's great; tell me what you're up to these days."

With that Samuelsson motioned to J.C. to have a seat on the couch and told the story of the rehab hospital, his recovery journey, the separation from his wife, his relationship with Marie, and his re-vision for the company, which J.C. found most interesting of all.

"I know I have to make a change in the way I do business. I've been more than a bit overbearing," he said.

J.C. wanted to high-five the CEO but kept his seat and just nodded slightly.

"That's why I wanted to talk to you. I really want to get feedback on myself from people who matter. Is that something you do?"

"Absolutely, I do it several ways in my relationship with a client."

Then J.C. went on to explain in detail just how he did that, including the 360 Continue-Stop-Start Evaluation.

J.C. explained that, to get to specific client behaviors, his 360-technique requires feedback from a variety of people — peers, direct reports and the person's supervisor. Each participant is chosen by the client as reliable and honest associates of the client, and they are asked three prime questions:

- What behavior(s) is the person being assessed exhibiting that s/he should *continue* to do to be even more successful?

- What behavior(s) should s/he *stop* in order to be even more successful?

- What behavior(s) should s/he *start* in order to be even more successful?

J.C. went on to explain that every respondent is granted anonymity and that after getting their collective feedback, he amalgamates all the responses into a summary and provides it back to the client. Sometimes the results are surprising, especially when clients are less self-aware.

When J.C. was finished, Stuart asked, "How long does it take?"

"About two weeks if people get back with the data promptly and I don't have to track them down to squeeze out the answers. That's why I always ask for more than I need for a snapshot."

"What do you usually find out?"

"That we often have a distorted sense of how others view us."

"Really?"

"We'll let the data stand on its own two feet and see."

They discussed how such a profile would help Samuelsson in the short term but would really be maximized if connected to an executive coaching engagement. Samuelsson thought that the idea had merit but wanted to first see how the 360 process worked and would then decide. J.C. agreed to the assignment and spent time collecting names from Samuelsson and asking him pointedly why each person on the list mattered to the CEO. J.C. told Samuelsson that he'd send over a contract in the afternoon and would start on the process when he got the down payment for this service. Both men shook hands, and J.C. headed to his next appointment.

Within a day, J.C. had a signed contract, and Samuelsson had sent out his introductory e-mail about J.C. working with him on self-assessment. J.C. sent out his e-mail with the data collection instrument attached and his offer to meet over the phone with anyone who needed any more information—and he set the deadline at one week.

Further in the note, he mentioned that their personal identification information would not be given and how important confidentiality was to the process.

He received two e-mails in reply that day from friends of Samuelsson who, as CEOs of other companies, were also his peers. Three more came in on Tuesday of the following week and by Friday, the deadline, he had all but two in. The two were from subordinates, whom J.C. called that day. One needed more assurances that his name would be held confidential, but in the end decided against it. The other had just forgotten and promised to get hers in that day.

The following week, J.C. arranged to present the data to Samuelsson, who had written up his own self-assessment. J.C. prepared the presentation using a flip chart. On one page he listed what Samuelsson had written in priority order. On the other page of the flip chart, J.C. posted the results of the survey he'd just conducted from stakeholders, whom Samuelsson had agreed were important to him and whose advice he would take seriously. All of this information would be revealed to Samuelsson at his office.

J.C. brought in the flip chart, set it on the easel that Marie had gotten for him, and proceeded with the presentation. He reviewed the process and explained that he had gotten seven of eight returns back and that one of the subordinates had not felt safe enough to return the form. However, because the data was so convincing and the majority of forms had been returned, J.C. did not see a need to ask Samuelsson for a substitute subordinate name. Samuelsson nodded in agreement, and J.C. turned over the blank page, revealing the data that Samuelsson himself had provided:

Continue:

1. Pushing hard for profitability
2. Being firm but fair
3. Staying focused on excellence

Stop:

1. Drinking (stay sober)
2. Demanding so much from people

Start:

1. Giving more bonuses
2. Increasing salaries

J.C. discussed these briefly in general terms because Samuelsson himself had provided the data. But J.C. had had experience with busy executives forgetting exactly what they had said, so he always offered their comments first before revealing the second sheet.

"That sounds right, as I recall," Samuelsson said.

"Good," J.C. said. "Now I'm going to show you what your seven of eight stakeholders, whom you said you respected, said in response to the same set of questions. Their answers, like yours, are in priority order and for confidentiality are aggregated, so you will not know who said what." Samuelsson nodded assent, and J.C. flipped over the next page:

Continue:

1. Staying sober
2. Working on your anger

Stop:

1. Worrying about money; it will come with team effort
2. Badgering people about numbers, stats, and minutiae

Start:

1. Encouraging employees; praising them for what they do
2. Showing personal interest in people

Samuelsson stared at the two lists, which by now J.C. had torn off the easel and had taped side by side on the wall.

	Client	Stakeholder
Continue	1. Pushing hard for profitability 2. Being firm but fair 3. Staying focused on excellence	1. Staying sober 2. Working on your anger
Stop	1. Drinking (stay sober) 2. Demanding so much from people	1. Worrying about money; it will come with team effort 2. Badgering people about numbers, stats, and minutiae
Start	1. Giving more bonuses 2. Increasing salaries	1. Encouraging employees; praising them for what they do 2. Showing personal interest in people

"What do you think?" J.C. asked.

"I'm confused and surprised."

"How so?"

"Well, the way I interpreted what I should stop—drinking—they saw as what I should continue to do . . . stay sober that is!"

J.C. chuckled and said, "So there you have a match, so let's put a plus by each of those," J.C. said adding a plus mark to both on the combined lists." Anything else jump out at you?"

"Yeah, money. I thought money might be the key incentive, and what I should start giving more of, but that doesn't even register on the stakeholders' radar."

"Yes, I agree," J.C. said, putting minus signs next to everything in the "START" boxes, on the client side. "Anything else?"

Samuelsson stared long and hard at the data. It had hit him like someone tossing a glass of cold water in his face. "Yes, it seems like people see me too worried about money and too little concerned about them."

"I would agree with your analysis."

"So where do we go from here?" Stuart asked, leaning toward J.C.

"We start coaching around the issues of over focusing on money and under focusing on people, if you'd like."

Samuelsson nodded assent and continued to stare at the charts.

Chapter 13:
Planting a New Tree

The next couple of months at SameTech1 were not easy for Ann Tabor. After she'd denied Brad the promotion, her relationship with him had turned cool and distant. He attended all required meetings but participated like a detached observer, not a team player. He did what he had to, not much more. And when the clock hit 5:00 p.m., he was out the door. Ann let it go for a while in order to allow him to grieve, but she was becoming more concerned that his performance was slipping and others were noticing as well.

She had regular contact with J.C., who asked her many pointed questions as he prodded but patiently waited for her to decide to do something. Finally, one day after a staff meeting, in which Brad had been especially detached and at times even belligerent, Ann asked him to remain behind after the others left.

"Brad, it's been two months since . . ."

"What?" he said with a tone that sounded like he wanted a fight.

"Since I told you that you didn't get the brand manager job. I know . . ."

He interrupted her. "You know what? What do you know?"

She took a deep breath and said, "You act like you're still deeply upset. That's what I know," she said, standing and walking around to the front of her desk. Now about two feet away from him, she stared directly at him. "I know you feel lousy, and I feel lousy. But, Brad, we have to get through this starting today. Do you understand that?"

Brad took a step back, and then another.

Ann continued, "And, frankly, I will not consider you for any other future promotion until you change your attitude."

He looked down at his feet.

"How you handle adversity and disappointment means a lot to me and so far, you're not showing me much," she said, almost not believing that she was hearing her own voice saying these words.

"I guess you're right," he said slowly, deliberately and softly.

"So how do we get past this?" she asked with her palms faced up.

"I guess one day at a time."

"Now that sounds like a plan," she said, reaching out her hand to shake his.

Chapter 14:
Cutting Through the Thicket

J.C. and Jane Smithfield had covered a lot of ground during the discovery phase, and so when J.C. met with her for the third time in her office at III-Tech, he had her fill out an instrument he called the "Balance Beam." It was a graph that asked clients to rate aspects of their lives on a scale that ranged from 0 to 100 percent. The bar graph looked straight, like a solid beam of wood, if someone were very balanced, or it looked warped with dips and rises in an imbalanced life. Jane's was more warped than straight. Her scores were typically high in career, money, and environment, but low in friends and family, fun and recreation, and significant others. J.C. wasn't surprised. Jane was a no-nonsense woman clearly focused on her business.

They had talked about her values—integrity, a strong work ethic, honesty, and responsibility—a good set of guideposts for a potential CEO. She had some trouble with a future visioning exercise he'd assigned her—to describe the perfect world in which she was doing everything that gave her energy. At first she took the assignment literally—so she answered with thoughts of food, water, sleep. But even after J.C. clarified the assignment and she'd revised her responses, she still had difficulty seeing the exercise as being of any help to her. After this third session together, while J.C. was still assembling the stakeholder responses from her 360 Continue-Stop-Start Evaluation, J.C. could tell she was getting a bit bored by the process.

"Jane, hang in there," he said. "I guarantee that when we get back the survey results, the pace of the coaching and the intensity will pick up." To which she answered, "Let's hope." J.C. just nodded and smiled, thinking to himself, *OK . . . just wait until next week.*

At the fourth meeting, as planned, J.C. compared the 360 feedback charts with her, just like he had with other clients. First he showed her chart, then the stakeholders' chart, side by side. For the first minute or two, she just stared. J.C. waited, then asked, "What do you see?"

"Some similarity, mostly disparity. People see me as honest and direct but also as harsh, self-centered, and unsociable."

"Anything else?"

"Yeah, they want me to think more strategically, less tactically, and to become a better communicator inside the company — walk around and talk to people directly. And they apparently want me out of the building to schmooze more."

Her last comments had a negative tone to them, J.C. thought. So he asked her to talk about her attitude toward what the stakeholders had said.

The rest of the fourth week was spent getting Jane to commit to studying the goals for the fifth session so that they could lay down some measurable objectives — to prove to herself and the CEO she'd made progress. Their first agreed-upon review session with the CEO would be in a month, and J.C. wanted her ready with concrete accomplishments.

At that fifth session, when he and Jane were settled comfortably in her office, J.C. said, "So have you looked at which one or two behavioral goals you want to work on first?"

"Yes," she said, with no hesitation. "I need to communicate better inside and outside the company, and I think I have to work on strategic thinking."

Looking at his notes, remembering what the CEO had said and the results of the 360 instrument, J.C. said, "I think you nailed it. I agree, so let's get started."

"How?"

"With some questions. First, what does better internal communication look like? Better yet, if you had a great year communicating internally — what would that look like?"

"I'm not sure what you mean."

"What would you see if you were a TV camera watching yourself communicate well with your staff?"

"I suppose I'd be walking around talking to people?"

"About what?"

"Work . . . products."

"Just work?"

"What else?"

"How about their interests and their families?"

"Yes, I guess that might be appropriate."

"Why so?"

"To show interest in them, personally?"

"Sounds right to me, but I'm not sure you're convinced. Let me ask you a question. Did you ever have a coach or teacher whom you really liked and who influenced you?"

She thought for a moment and then said, "Mrs. Richardson, my high school chemistry teacher."

"Why?"

"She worked me hard and made me enter the science fair, which I eventually won."

"Is that it? She worked you hard?"

"No, she stayed after school and helped me complete the project. She even helped me get it home a few nights . . . it was a big ark of a thing on the effect of tides on the chemistry of the ecosphere."

"So, she did more than just teach you chemistry."

"Yes. Actually, I think of her, even today, like she was an aunt of mine—a smart aunt."

"Are you still in touch?"

"As a matter of fact, I send her a holiday card every year, and she sends me one."

"Do you do that with any other teacher you had, say at Harvard or MIT?"

"No."

"What's that say about Mrs. Richardson?"

"She became special to me."

"How so?"

"As someone who cared about me."

"Bingo!"

"The game?"

"No, I'm sorry. Bingo—as in 'you got it.'"

"I'm not following your analogy."

"Mrs. Richardson had become a teacher who really cared about you as a person. And that personal connection has meant all the difference in your relationship."

"Ah. Now I see."

"So, how can you become like Mrs. Richardson to your key employees?"

"I can get to know them personally as well as professionally?"

"OK, good. What else?"

"I can work with them on their future plans," she said more quickly and now without hesitation.

"Yes."

"I can make sure they have what they need to get their work done."

"Yes."

At this point Jane was rolling, even flooding, with ideas about how to communicate better one-on-one.

Working with a flip chart, Jane and J.C. started to make a grid:

My Personal Action Plan

Goal #1: To become a much better internal communicator

Action *What I need to do*	Standard *How I need to do it*	Timing *When I need to do it*	Results *Positive effect on business (or loss if not done)*
Meet with each of 10 direct reports.	Talk about job, interests, family for at least 10 minutes.	Weekly	Get to know what's on people's minds. Build personal connections.
Walk around the entire business every day.	Engage two people daily for 10 minutes.	Daily	Build better atmosphere — climate to flourish.
Develop an activities committee.	Fund a group to have social events at company.	Quarterly	Establish social traditions inside company . . . to help build new climate of camaraderie.

They also sketched out Goal #2: To become a better external communicator. Finally they worked on Goal #3: To become a better strategic thinker, which confused her a bit. So she and J.C. brainstormed.

"Let's start with football, which you told me before that you enjoy watching, especially college football." She nodded, so J.C. continued, "Let's say Harvard is playing Yale for their big game of the year, and you're the coach for Harvard."

"I like this game already," she said with a smile that seemed less difficult for her than before.

"What's your strategy?"

"To win."

"I'd say that's your big, overarching goal, but in large strokes how do you plan on executing on the goal— winning?"

"On offense, we'll use the running game to set up a passing attack."

"OK. Draw in the linebackers and then pass over them. I like that approach. How about defense?"

"Rattle Yale's new sophomore quarterback."

"You know more about football than I thought."

"I follow it closely, and Yale lost their senior, experienced QB in their last game, so they're vulnerable."

"I'd say you now have a good strategy. What you begin to do then is fill in the bullets below to load the strategy with actions—those are your tactics."

"So to rattle the rookie QB, we use blitzes, multiple formations, and frequent substitutions?"

"Yeah, you *do things*—tactics—to produce an overall effect—rattling the rookie quarterback."

Then she piped up, "I get it. Think big picture for strategy and more specific steps for tactics."

"Yeah, that's it in a nutshell."

"What happens if he doesn't rattle?" she said, challenging J.C. in a good-natured way.

"Simple, try a new strategy," J.C. said, smiling at her.

Chapter 15:
A Storm Brews in the Forest

Out of character, Liz Penrith was the first one to arrive at J.C.'s office for their monthly peer-group meeting. And when J.C. went to hug her, she broke down and cried into his shoulder.

"Hey, hey, what's going on?"

"I, we . . . I," she said and then heaved deeply and continued to cry.

He held her for some time and rocked gently as you might comfort a young child who wakes up with a bad dream. He knew it had to be something big because Liz was such a let-it-roll-off-your-back kind of person. Eventually, she raised her head and wiped her eyes, looked up at J.C., and said, "Ed wants a separation." Then she burst into a second wave of sobbing.

When Allison walked in and saw J.C. sitting on the couch gently rocking Liz, it took her by surprise. But J.C. looked her in the eyes, shook his head, motioning for her to be quiet. Liz had fallen asleep, probably because she hadn't slept well, if at all, last night, he surmised.

After Liz woke up, she provided the teary history of her and Ed's difficulties. Ed, a professor at the local university, had been working on a major research project for the past year with a young, attractive graduate student, with whom he had apparently fallen in love and intended to marry sooner rather than later—so he was going to file for divorce. Both J.C. and Allison were stunned because, having heard of Liz's life through her eyes, they'd thought that she and Ed lived in Camelot. They took trips, celebrated birthdays and holidays, and went to country fairs. Evidently, Ed was also interested in other pastimes and had conveniently forgotten to tell Liz.

"What should I do?"

Allison spoke first, "Get some counseling."

"You are my counselors, for God's sake."

"Not on this one. We're your friends and will always be your friends. But you and Ed need some professional counseling," J.C. said.

"Come on, we've walked each other through the toughest executive situations anyone can imagine. You remember that CEO who got arrested for drunk and disorderly and had to explain his extracurricular activities to his board?"

"Yeah, but that was coaching, not counseling. You'll recall after that incident, I recommended that he start to see a counselor, and I ended my engagement with him because I thought he needed counseling more . . . it was in his best interest," J.C. said.

"Yeah, and you gave up a pretty healthy monthly retainer to do it, as I recall," Allison said.

J.C. nodded and said, "What you, Ed, and your daughter are facing requires a marriage counselor, not an executive coach."

Liz began to cry again. Finally she said, "I know, but you guys are my most trusted friends in the world."

"And we'll always support you and be your friends. You know that. We just can't ethically be your counselors," J.C. said.

"I know."

For the rest of their monthly meeting, they talked about Liz's situation. She explained that Ed had started to act strangely about six months into the new research project he was working on. He had mentioned the team and even spoke about his brilliant doctoral student, Amy. Then the team started to travel to several different sites and after the third trip or so, Ed started acting colder toward Liz and quicker to argue with her about her thrift-store dressing, her constant lateness, her overly humorous demeanor, her scatter-brained personality . . . everything he'd originally found so attractive. One night he had worked late in the basement on his computer, had fallen asleep on the basement couch, and left on his e-mail. When Liz went down to the basement and was about to turn off the lights and his computer, she saw a header at the top of his incoming e-mail, from Amy, captioned, "Love you!"

Liz's curiosity got the best of her and she opened it. She learned they'd been exchanging love notes for some time. Liz told J.C. and Allison how utterly devastated she became, how she confronted Ed, how he denied it, how she showed him a copy of the e-mail, how he railed at her for invasion of privacy, how they argued, how he ended up leaving the next day . . . how her life had changed so quickly.

Allison and J.C. consoled her and gave her some tea. J.C. called a marriage counselor to set up an appointment for his friend, and then they put her in her car. After that J.C. and Allison sat together in his office.

"How awful," Allison said.

"Yes. I feel so bad for Liz."

"Could that be us one day?" she said moving closer to J.C.

"I certainly hope not," he said drawing her into his shoulder.

Chapter 16:
Tree Trimming

For the past six weeks, J.C. had been meeting with David Blackmon for an hour a week, offering what J.C. called "sounding board" coaching, where he listened and responded to what David had experienced in the past week. J.C. believed that David needed an intense, quick-start kind of coaching that focused on the short term, rather than long term—or by then David might no longer be the executive director of the foundation.

Every session started with J.C. simply asking David one question: "So what's going on?" That triggered the extroverted client to start, stopping only when J.C. offered any one of many clarifying questions, such as:

How so?

What does that mean?

How did that make you feel?

What did he or she say in response?

What was the result of that conversation?

What is it that you really want?

What will it take for you to change that?

What conversations do you need to have with whomever to get the results you want?

Where could you better leverage your strengths?

Also, during their second meeting, to accelerate the coaching process, J.C. had decided to employ a very risky tactic because he didn't believe that David knew the severity of his situation and because J.C. knew just how upset Max was with David. So, soon after they had sat down and David had begun his rambling, self-serving monologue following J.C.'s opening question, J.C. held up his hand like a traffic cop and said, "STOP for a moment, please." It took David 20 or 30 seconds and a second, "Please STOP" before he stopped.

David looked more surprised than angry, and J.C. pulled his hand down. Clasping it loosely with his other hand, he leaned forward, saying, "I'm going to be brutally honest with you, OK?"

David nodded in an almost dismissive manner.

J.C. began slowly. "You were referred to me by your Board of Directors," he said. "They believe that you bring certain valuable gifts to the table. You're smart, connected, attractive—all of which help in raising money, a big part of your job."

David seemed to settle back into a confident state as he waited for the other shoe to drop.

"Along with all that, you have another responsibility— to work with your Board of Directors," J.C. added. "On this matter, they are less than satisfied."

Both just stared at each other. Finally David spoke. "Go on."

J.C. continued, now leaning back in his chair with a voice that was slower and less urgent. "Look, most CEOs are successful because they have a set of traits including the courage to set off on a course when others don't quite see where they're going," he said. "Often the very traits that make them great can be their undoing, when carried to extremes; also their inferiors can take them down a destructive path—actually derail them."

"Inferiors?"

"People have strengths, which means the opposites are their inferiors—it's a Jungian thing."

"As in Carl Jung?"

"Yep . . . but let's not get hung up on theory. Simply— you're a very outgoing guy. You speak well—you're articulate and influential — real strengths. When you overdo that, you come off as slick, overdone, a bit untrustworthy. That's an example of a strength derailing your success train."

"Alright, how about the opposite, inferior thing?"

"The opposite of an extroversion is introversion — introspection, thinking before you talk, trusting your inner voice and, in short, taking a deep breath and counting to 10 — or 20 or 30 — before you respond. Especially, especially, when you're angry or frustrated."

"Are you referring to that time I called the Board small minded and lethargic?"

"You actually said that to your entire Board — in a public setting?" J.C. was incredulous.

"Well, they could not see the clear path I had laid out in a very logical strategic plan — which was vetted by MC Lamb — the best strategic consulting firm in the country. My cousin works there as a senior partner. He and several of his colleagues reviewed my plan and said it was the best they'd ever seen. *But* my Board wanted a local hack of a consultant to sign off on it first. Absolutely ridiculous!"

"Maybe in your mind, but not in your Board's opinion. Let's roleplay for a minute."

"Must we?"

"Humor me. I'd like you pretend that you're a Marine company commander in Iraq. Your company has one platoon pinned down. You have to get them out, or they'll all be captured or killed. You know that the insurgents are planning to beef up the attack and are coming in from a deserted back road dressed as civilians, but you don't have time to explain everything in detail because the events are unfolding very fast, and it is a most dangerous situation. You tell another platoon commander to move his troops away from the action to a preset alternative position that you know will place them in the path of the infiltrating insurgents but takes them out of the direct action for a while. But the lieutenant in charge of that maneuvering platoon thinks you're small minded and incompetent and that you just don't understand strategy, so he refuses to leave the action. What would you do?"

"Relieve him of his command and place a sergeant in charge."

"Bingo . . . now do you get it?"

Their conversation lasted an hour more than scheduled because J.C. believed they'd had a significant "break-through" or "Aha!" moment and didn't want to lose the momentum. During the course of most executive coaching engagements, J.C. had such breakthrough moments, usually following one uncomfortable confrontation or other. Sometimes it was immediate; other times there was a delayed reaction. Sometimes it took the client on the path toward success, and sometimes it did not. J.C. hoped for the best with David.

As their conversation proceeded, when David got off on a tangent or tirade, J.C. interrupted him and pulled him back to the question he needed answered. In other cases when time was running short, J.C. would summarize the engagement and offer his observations by saying, "OK. Let me summarize what you've said and see if I have it straight. . . ."

At particularly poignant times, J.C. had to ask permission to go from being a coach or sounding board to being a consultant offering a strong opinion, even advice. For example, at one point David was on a rant about how unintelligent and out of touch Max Ingersoll was.

"May I speak very directly to you at this point?" J.C. asked, leaning forward and staring at David.

"OK."

"You are *way* off base. Max has started and run three very successful businesses and taken two of them public; he is a graduate of Harvard Law School and has an MBA from Wharton. Those are just a few of his many accomplishments. Just read your own Foundation Web page. For you to discount him as either unintelligent or out of touch is frankly unjustifiable and inaccurate."

After another 15 minutes of discussion, they ended the session, both frankly exhausted by the energy that such confrontations take. But before he left, David made sure to confirm their meeting for the following week.

Chapter 17:
Cutting a New Path

Meeting each week for an hour either by phone or in person, J.C. and Stuart Samuelsson worked together for a month. During that period, J.C. had asked Samuelsson to engage in a process that J.C. called fast-forward to make progress on a specific behavioral objective. Samuelsson had agreed to work on not being overbearing—not riding employees unmercifully about the bottom line. Time and again that theme had surfaced in his 360 evaluation.

J.C. agreed with the objective but wanted to put some qualitative and quantitative measures on it so that both he and Samuelsson could define and achieve success. Samuelsson laughed at first, as much at his personal problem as at any method to evaluate it, and said, "And just how do we measure badgering abatement?"

"By asking those being badgered."

"Hmm."

"Actually, it's not as difficult as it might sound. I call the technique fast-forward."

"As in a tape recorder?"

"Not quite. The idea is that most people remember what happened in the past and often raise it in an annual evaluation—you-did-this or didn't-do-that sort of stuff. The problem is that such feed*back* is archeology—digging up the past. In an annual evaluation it ends up feeling more accusatory—more blameful than helpful."

"Then my ex-wife was an expert at feedback! She could remember something I did 10 years ago—with incredible specificity."

"And how did that make you feel?"

"Angry. What the hell could I do about something I did over a decade ago?" he said, shrugging his shoulders and looking toward the ceiling.

"Exactly. And that's precisely how employees feel at performance appraisal time. If we like what they've done, we pick out a few good examples, rate them high, and sign the plan for the next year."

"Yep . . . pretty useless."

"Unless they're somehow combined with moving forward—and doing the appraisals every month or two along the way."

"That's a lot of time."

"Perhaps a bit more time, but the payoff is so great. Let me explain how we're going to test the same sort of process out on you."

"OK."

"I'm going to ask you to talk to every stakeholder who responded to your 360 evaluation. Actually, I'll give you the entire list even though one person did not respond. It won't matter. If you approach them correctly, they'll all help you."

"I admire your confidence, but . . ."

J.C. interrupted, "No buts for now."

Samuelsson looked a bit stunned but nodded toward his young coach, whom he'd begun to admire.

"So," J.C. continued, "here's how fast-forward works. You'll send them all individually an e-mail explaining that while you don't know who said what in your 360 evaluation, the aggregate data indicated a number of useful observations, especially about your behavior, that you want to change—specifically, you're interested in not badgering employees so much about the bottom line. You'll explain that for the next few months, this will be your biggest goal, and you'd like their help in moving forward. You'll meet with them in the next week and seek out just what you can do to meet that goal and report back every few weeks to let them know how you're doing."

"And what do you think their response will be?"

"They'll give it a try, but if you debate with them, fail to follow up on their suggestions, or fail to tell them what you're doing specifically to improve, the whole thing goes down the drain. In short, you have to be patient, listen, and do something."

"In other words don't badger them about curbing my badgering!"

Both he and J.C. laughed.

"Exactly. But there's more. The stakeholders have responsibilities, too, and I'll give you language you can use in your e-mail. Here's the shorthand version," he said, reaching for a note card so that he could write it down for Stuart.

Stakeholder Fast-Forward

1. Tell me how I do things right in the future, not what I did wrong in the past.
2. Don't expect perfection, but *do* expect an honest effort.
3. Be willing to notice small changes in the right direction.
4. Be positive, not negative—be supportive, not cynical. Become coaches, *not* just spectators.
5. Participate in my periodic evaluations, which my coach will send to you.

Stuart chimed in, "Most of these I understand, but explain to me the evaluation process."

"I'll explain that later. Now go forth and do it—fast-forward."

Chapter 18:
Reading the Compass in the Woods

J.C. had been working with Jane Smithfield, the prospective CEO of III-Tech, for several months. She had absorbed her 360 evaluation and chosen to work on her first area—better internal communications. When J.C. arrived for his now twice-a-month, one- to two-hour session, he sat in Jane's office with the chart they had laid out several months ago to do a pre-evaluation of her goal. She had written in red her actual accomplishments. But before they went through the chart, J.C. asked her how she felt.

"Different—in a little better way. I'm more in touch with what's really going on in the company. I think the walking around—knowing I have to speak to two people a day—helped prime the pump."

"Good, anything else?"

"Yes, in my fast-forward sessions, I've been getting a lot of good tips about building personal relationships at work."

"Like what, for instance?"

"Simple things like bringing back a coffee to someone when I go out to Starbucks in the afternoon, or sending a birthday card—simple acts of kindness. Nothing huge, but the effects are extraordinary. Everyone tries to pay you back by doing at least the same amount of effort—often more. Two weeks ago, a few of the staff bought me a birthday cake and flowers. I was astonished."

"Sounds like you're making great progress. This doesn't surprise me at all. Let's look at your chart here," he said, pointing at the grid in front of them both.

Goal #1: Improve Internal Communications

Action	Standard	Timing	Desired Results *positive effect on business or loss if not done*	Actual Action	Results
Meet with each of 10 direct reports.	Talk about job, interests, family for at least 10 minutes.	Weekly	Get to know what's on people's minds. Build personal connections.	Met with 8 people for 10 minutes about themselves, not just business . . . see attached for list	– Mary sent birthday card – Jason brought me coffee – Melissa confided in me on work issue
Walk around the entire business every day.	Engage two people about the business throughout company.	Daily	Build better atmosphere— climate to flourish.	Engaged an average of 2.5 people/day	– Staff meeting went better – Planning off-site – Asked to join softball team
Develop an activities committee.	Fund a group to have social events at company.	Quarterly	Establish social traditions inside company . . . to help build new climate of camaraderie.	– Funded new activities committee – Sought volunteers	– Hosted first party – Planning list of year's events
Start a monthly employee newsletter.	In two months, publish the first employee newsletter.	Monthly	Improve internal employee recognition and communication.	– Sent e-mail to solicit group – Met with and established working group – Set schedule for publication	– All-employee e-mail survey got high marks – Publication team is meeting after work to write first edition

He looked at the chart and nodded his head approvingly. Then, she flipped to the second page on the chart to Goal #2: To Improve External Communications. Again, she hit, or nearly hit, all her specific objectives and had filled out the boxes. Then she turned to the final page — Goal #3: Engage in More Strategic Thinking. Her chart here showed that she had enrolled in a course at a local university and had worked directly with the CEO on planning the next board meeting focused on strategic branding for the company. Further, according to her chart, she was now also devoting a significant amount of her day to focusing on strategic goals that she and the CEO had agreed upon beforehand.

Throughout Jane's enthusiastic monologue, J.C. mostly listened and smiled. It was clear to J.C. that she had made changes and people were noticing.

"Now we evaluate."

"How's that work?"

"Actually, based on all you've done, this part is easy and painless, and reveals a lot. Early next week, I'll send out a simple two- or three-item questionnaire that I'll ask your stakeholders to fill out." He took out a blank index card from his pocket and drew the following chart:

1. Jane has shown concrete behavioral change when interacting with people inside the company more positively.

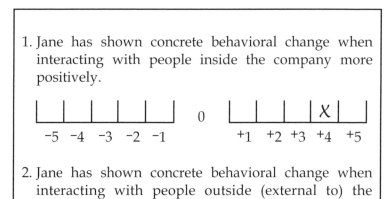

2. Jane has shown concrete behavioral change when interacting with people outside (external to) the company more positively.

3. Jane has exhibited more strategic behavior in the past several months.

4. Any additional comments/observations you'd like to add?

_____

_____

"This is what it will look like, and your stakeholders will simply insert an X in the appropriate box. A "+3" indicates that you're making moderate, but positive movement toward your goal. A "-4" would mean that you had gotten significantly worse."

"In that case, I'd be a candidate for exile, in other words!"

J.C. laughed and said, "Let's assume if you do things right, you'll be pushing more toward the good leader, rather than the dictator—ready to be overthrown by the angry mob."

"Let's hope for the best!" she blurted out with more excitement than J.C. had ever seen her display before.

Chapter 19:
A Campfire Chat in the Woods

Liz arrived on time for their monthly meeting only to find out that Allison would not be attending—one of her clients had a problem she had to address. She had called J.C. and explained the situation and sent her regrets.

"I'm sorry Allison's not going to get to hear my great report."

"So tell me," said J.C.

Liz went on to explain that after her separation and recent quick divorce, pushed by her ex-husband, she'd met a great new guy. They'd fallen in love, and she couldn't believe it. But she'd been talking to her therapist about not doing anything permanent for a while to let the new love settle in—to avoid rebounding. Nonetheless, she was on top of life. Her business was thriving, her child was happy and healthy, and as for her love life, "ooh-la-la" was how she described it.

"How about you, J.C.?"

"It's all good."

"Define *all* and *good.*"

"I'm fine."

"How about you and Allison?"

"I'd rather keep that between us."

Liz prodded and poked and used every technique she could to get J.C. to tell her about where his relationship with Allison was headed. But he would not budge. Frustrated, she brought up the elephant in the room. "How's your cancer? Does it scare you away from relationships?"

"Liz, be careful. You're a friend. Don't push it," he said as his face flushed.

"I'm sorry, J.C., but you're always helping others break through. And we all know that only happens when something's at stake. So I'm asking you as a friend . . . what's up with your health?"

He turned away from her to grab a glass of wine, but stayed turned longer than necessary. Liz saw him wipe his right eye quickly, faking that something had gotten into it.

"J.C., please?"

He started to talk with his head turned away from her, "The doctors at Johns Hopkins can't tell if it's under control fully or still metastasizing. I'm still losing weight and my blood is anemic."

"I'm sorry."

By now he had turned toward her, and the dark streak that had run down the side of his cheek betrayed him. "Me too."

"What does Allison say?"

"She's not afraid at all. But . . ."

"But you are? For her, I mean?"

"I'm feeling pretty selfish these days."

"Selfish. Why?"

"I might leave on any day. She deserves better."

"Isn't that her choice?"

They talked for an hour after their usual stopping time when finally the door opened, and Allison entered. She looked at the two of them and said, "Hey, what's going on?"

They both looked at her and said almost in chorus, "Nothing."

"OK, that means we really need to talk then."

Chapter 20:
Deadwood

The phone call came from Max Ingersoll the evening before J.C. was to meet with David Blackmon for one of their weekly "sounding board" meetings.

"J.C., I'm sorry to call so late in the evening, but I wanted to fill you in as soon as possible."

"Sure . . . what's up?"

"With the concurrence—a unanimous vote—from the board, I fired David Blackmon." The words hung in the phone like sand suspended in a turbulent surf. *David Blackmon, fired.* Then two thoughts crowded his mind. Good. And bad. Good—because he'd always wanted to see David disciplined like a spoiled, silver-spooned brat. Bad—because David at least was working on himself, and J.C. hated to lose a client before he'd finished his job of coaching them to achieve success.

"I see. What happened?"

"As you know, we have a donor-advised fund. That means donors tell us their wishes as to where they'd like their money to go. We advise them if we believe it is misdirected, but we generally try to see the donor's wishes through unless we see them going well off course. Then we put our foot down because technically the money is ours to invest in the community."

"I see."

"One of our largest donors is a bit of a pain, but he's worth the effort because of what he does for the community. For example, every year he gives $100,000 in unrestricted funds to the open fund for community projects, which the board doles out annually. Truly, it's the best part of my job as chairman every year—to grant that money directly to the community."

"So what happened?"

"Basically, in my mind and the board's, David got into a heated, and I might say unnecessary, battle with this donor over trivial matters."

"Like what?"

Max went on to explain that David had told the donor that he was wasting his time and money sending it to a local charity that David found less than worthy, and that he would not recommend board approval of his donation to the organization. It so happened that the donor had already promised the charity's CEO the money and would not back off the promise. The argument escalated into an e-mail flame war in which David used words such as "silly," "immature," "inane," and others, all of which were later shown to the entire board in a closed executive session by the long-time donor who was appalled at the way he'd been treated.

This meeting came on the heels of several complaints from the public and from members of the board. All this negative feedback prompted the board to demand that Max call a vote to remove David. Frankly, Max was surprised when the vote became unanimous.

"After the donor left, we called in David," he told J.C. "We explained that his actions in the past year had been inappropriate. The way he treated the most recent donor was so far off-base it had to be discussed directly by the board with the donor. We told David that the executive board had voted unanimously to fire him."

"What did he say?"

"He brushed it aside as if I had told him the temperature outside was 65 degrees."

"And what did you do then?"

"I called the COO into the meeting and appointed him interim executive director, and asked that security escort David out of the building."

Later that afternoon, J.C. tried to reach David on his cell phone, but he was not picking up. J.C. sent e-mails and left calls. Nothing. After a few weeks, J.C. learned that David had taken a job with his father's firm.

J.C. felt like a doctor who had just lost a patient.

Chapter 21:
Springtime in the Forest

Stuart Samuelsson's voice on the phone was almost giddy. "Can you meet me for lunch today? I have some good news. Great news, in fact."

J.C. met Stuart at their regular haunt not far from Stuart's office. Stuart was already seated and tapping a pad of paper with his pen. When J.C. sat down, Stuart started out with one bombshell after another.

"Well, first, Marie and I have decided to get married!" he said with a smile that enveloped his face.

"Congratulations, Stuart. She's a great woman, and you both seem so happy together. Besides, she's seen you through some real ups and downs."

"You can say that . . . especially when I was in the hospital and rehab. But it's been a year now, and I've been clean and sober."

"Yes, and I'm proud of what you've accomplished."

"One day at a time."

J.C. nodded a kind of silent *amen* and said, "Well, let's toast our waters to that."

"In just a minute. I have more news," he said as he paused, "The board has elected me to be chairman and CEO."

"What a nice vote of confidence. A long way from a year ago."

"Yep. And that's not all. I talked to Jack."

"Jack?"

"Jack Wilhelm—my former COO. Who became CEO of a competitor of ours. When he left, he said it was a great opportunity, but I knew better. He left because I was such a jerk."

J.C. laughed and slapped his knee. "Your words, not mine."

"I've talked him into coming back as our president for a year and then if all goes well to becoming CEO, when I move to full-time chairman."

"Wow. What a red-letter day for you. Three big ones. I hope you can handle all that good fortune at once!"

"I'll try. And I want to thank you for taking me on as a client. You've helped me . . . a lot. Marie was the best thing that ever happened to me. Jack's back . . . all's right with the world."

"Hear! Hear!" J.C. said, lifting up his water glass to toast his friend and colleague.

*****

The next week, J.C. got a call from Sam Adams asking if J.C. could stop by the office. When J.C. arrived, both Sam and Jane Smithfield were seated, having a conversation.

"Oh, J.C., come on in. Jane and I were just talking about you."

"All good, I hope. No voodoo dolls and pins?"

Jane and Sam laughed as Sam motioned J.C. toward a comfortable chair near the conversation area. Spread out on the coffee table in front of where Sam and Jane had been sitting were pictures of a quaint cottage situated in the midst of a treed lot. Some shots showed the woods, and others showed the dock along a wide river and a sailboat tied up to the dock.

Sam pointed to the cottage and said, "J.C., here's my new home. How do you like it?"

"It's beautiful, but I didn't know you were moving."

"Well, I'm not entirely, but I will be spending much more time on the river. I plan on writing, which I've always complained I didn't have enough time for, and I want to use the cottage as a place for my grandkids to enjoy."

"Wonderful," said J.C.

"The rest of the story, as Paul Harvey might say, is that Jane will be taking over as CEO."

As he said the words for the first time to a third party, Sam beamed. Jane lit up as well, in an almost embarrassed way, and J.C. exclaimed, "Terrific . . . that's just terrific. I'm so glad for both of you."

"And we're thankful to you for all your help in making this possible," Jane said. "Without your help, I'm not sure I could have ever gotten here." Sam nodded as he sipped his coffee.

"I do appreciate your thanks and thank you both as well for sticking with me throughout the process. It was a lot of work but, Jane, you stuck with it, and Sam, you paid for it!" he said smiling at them both.

Sam then spoke, "We're both so grateful for your excellent coaching that we wanted to do something for you—something you could use and that might be fun. So Jane and I split a gift for you . . . well, a gift in your name, to be more precise," he said, handing J.C. an envelope that had his name on it.

J.C. looked a little bewildered as he opened the letter and read. He took a moment to reread it and then looked up at them both and said, "Wow. A scholarship in my name at UVa! I'm speechless, really."

"I doubt that will be for long," Jane said as both she and Sam laughed.

*****

Months later at one of their regular meetings, Liz beamed. As she pulled her left hand from around her back, she pointed at a beautiful diamond ring. "Tony?" Allison asked.

"Yep, nice taste, huh? In rings and women," Liz said.

"I can't believe how far you've come. It's amazing. And you did it with such style and class."

"And a lot of help from my friends," she said, pointing at them both, "and a good therapist. Monica was such a great find. Thanks, J.C., I can never repay you for the referral. She got me through some very dark days and out into the sunlight. I'm so eternally grateful."

"You're a friend. I was glad to help. You'd do the same for me, I know."

"You bet. Just try me."

"I hope not under similar circumstances," J.C. said laughing and pointing at Allison.

"No, indeed," Liz said and smiled at J.C.

Chapter 22:
What Is Executive Coaching?

As long as there have been good listeners and trusted advisors in the executive suite, there have been executive coaches. Not all executive coaches are trained, paid, or even know they're coaches, for that matter. Indeed, when coaching is done well, it looks more like a good friend listening and asking probing questions and less like a football coach barking orders—in fact, the very opposite. So, the term *coaching,* while widely used, is a bit misleading. We should be called executive facilitators . . . but that just doesn't have any panache. So, executive coach it remains.

The coaching process begins when the client realizes that he or she wants help getting to the next level of performance. Often, the organization (the director of Human Resources, CEO, or chairperson) will not only initiate the process but also pay for it. Ultimately, however, the relationship between the client and the coach is the primary and principal relationship—one that remains confidential . . . though not protected by law in the same way lawyers and doctors and their clients enjoy that privilege. Yet the spirit of confidentiality is as vital to the coaching relationship as in any other profession—including law and medicine.

What follows is an explication of the coaching process to help you understand it better. While each step is distinct, together they are part of a whole process that is executive coaching. You may remember reading some of this in the chapter where J.C. explained the main steps to his new client, Jane Smithfield.

Step One — Pre-Coaching

Formal coaching really begins with a phase known as Pre-Coaching interviews. These interviews are often held with the CEO or Human Resources department. The purpose is to identify the executive to be coached.

At this meeting, I listen carefully to why the company wants coaching for the executive. For example, if the company is using coaching as a last ditch, do-or-die, retain-or-fire solution, then I often refuse the offer to coach because coaching is about moving forward, not termination. If the organization wants the best for the executive, I'm open to the next interview, which is with the executive.

During this interview, I ask a lot of questions, mostly centered on why the executive thinks he or she might want coaching and why it's being sought at this specific time. I explain what coaching is and how it works, and then describe the general commitment to the entire process, which takes both time and energy. I also get a sense very quickly about whether or not chemistry exists between the executive and me (or as Malcolm Gladwell refers to it in his book *Blink,* "thin slicing"). Clients and coaches either click or they don't, and this click usually happens quickly. If the meetings with both the executive and management go well, I typically sign a contract for six months or a year with the client and the company.

In the story, J.C. had several pre-coaching interviews, and two of them indicated existing problems. His first get-acquainted interview with Stuart Samuelsson ended "in a huff," but left the ball in Samuelsson's court. J.C. knew from the outset that Samuelsson's problem was deep and well hidden. Turns out J.C. was right — Samuelsson was an alcoholic, was having an affair with his secretary, and was not at the "coachable moment" in his life — not yet. The pre-coaching interview with David Blackmon was a disaster from the start—Blackmon arrived a half-hour late, never apologized, and acted arrogantly, so J.C. walked out on him. Were it not for the follow-up and insistence of Max Ingersoll, Blackmon's chairman, J.C. would never have continued. J.C. did continue, but the overwhelming hubris that Blackmon presented in the pre-coaching interview eventually became his complete undoing and by extension, the end of the coaching relationship.

Step Two—Self-Discovery and Awareness

The second phase of the coaching process begins with an initial session, which often lasts two hours and which I conduct face-to-face. During this meeting, the client and I discuss what coaching is and how it's different from consulting. I explain that consultants typically have expert answers, but that coaches have lots of probing questions with the belief that the client ultimately holds all the answers. We also discuss the following points:

- Coaching takes time, energy, and commitment from the client in order to work.

- The coach–client relationship is confidential, and I will not reveal the identity or contents of the coaching sessions without permission from the client. In the event that the organization or board wants a progress report about the coaching, I encourage the client to debrief them directly. Short of that, I will only discuss—in very general terms—progress toward goal attainment and overall client engagement in the process, and only with permission from the client.

- Coaching has a rhythm; it ebbs and flows, typically "dipping" after the first few months as the work sets in and the excitement wanes. Clients need to be aware of this normal process in order to manage their early expectations.

- There is a big difference between coaching and counseling. Whereas coaching deals with concerned clients addressing work-related behavioral issues, counseling is the purview of trained psychologists and psychiatrists, who work with an individual's physiological, psychological, and emotional challenges. In fact, when I see a client with physical or psychological problems that would be better treated by other professionals, I'm ethically obligated to cease coaching and refer the client to an appropriate professional.

- In the coaching process, we work on identifying those inner voices in all of us that want to maintain the safer, more familiar status quo. We also discuss how to recognize such inhibiting voices as "We've always done it that way," or "We tried that before, and it didn't work," or "Same old story, different day." Identifying these voices before the coaching starts helps both the client and coach recognize them and gives them a name when they rear their heads—as they always do. You may recall in the story how J.C. identified some of Jane's nagging inner voices like "I'm fine" and "Whatever."

- Setting up our relationship for success will involve assignments and readings. As in all one-on-one interactions, we'll likely come up against personal likes and dislikes and a number of other issues. Notice how Ann Tabor had to confront her professional issue of not being able to say "No" to people because she wanted to be well liked.

- The process of the coaching engagement spans everything from goal setting to assigned practices, and we discuss the duration, format, and frequency of our work together.

- We'll also spend some time getting in touch with the value proposition for the client and the potential business impact if he or she does or does not achieve the goals of the coaching engagement.

For a good example of this part of the discovery phase, take a look at how J.C. and Jane Smithfield interact in their early meeting. In that scene you have a realistic view of what an initial meeting looks like, as the client begins to absorb the reality of what coaching is all about. Initially, most people I coach don't have an in-depth grasp of the coaching process. I think that's largely the profession's shortcoming—not having talked in more detail about the process—which is why I wrote this book. Many clients come into the first meeting having only a vague idea of what coaching is. So when they start getting into the nitty-gritty details, there's always some healthy tension that accompanies the meeting.

During the next part of the Self-Discovery and Awareness phase, which will last for several weeks, I ask clients to work on several instruments and exercises: the balance beam that looks at where they're content with or discontented with their lives; Strengths Finder indicator reference from the book *Discover Your Strengths* by Marcus Buckingham and Donald Clifton; an exercise in which they write a short autobiography of themselves; and several other exercises that will give me insight into them — and give them insight into themselves.

Finally, in this phase, if they are willing, I offer the clients the option of having a 360-degree evaluation. Sometimes, the CEO, HR, and the client agree up front on what behavioral aspects they want covered in the coaching — so the 360, which might well be helpful, is unnecessary at this point, but might be relevant later depending on what the client and sponsor would like as the relationship grows.

There are a number of 360 evaluations available on the market. Many are extremely well researched, reliable, and data driven. Some produce prodigious reports and often with specific remedies for the client. Given time and the option, I prefer to do a more qualitative 360 evaluation, which I call "The 360 Continue-Stop-Start." I ask the client to give me a list of six to eight people who are their direct reports, peers, and the supervisor (boss). Then, the client notifies them that I'll be sending them an instrument to fill out and return to me (the coach). I assure them that the data will be aggregated so as to protect the identity of each stakeholder and specifically of who said what. I also ask the client to fill out the same instrument so that we can compare the stakeholder aggregate perception data with the client perception data. The contrast is often startling for clients and a great place to start working on behavioral issues.

The 360 process was demonstrated when Samuelsson agreed to do a 360 evaluation. Samuelsson thought that he was good at and should "continue" to stay focused on profitability and excellent but his stakeholders suggested that he "continue" staying other and working on anger management — quite different gs.

no

Samuelsson thought he should "stop" drinking and "stop" demanding so much from people. His stakeholders thought he should "stop" obsessing about money and badgering people about minutiae. Finally, Samuelsson thought he should "start" giving more bonuses and pay raises, but his stakeholders thought he should "start" praising people and "start" showing that he cared about them as people.

After reviewing the comparison between how clients view themselves and how significant (client-chosen) stakeholders view clients, we begin specific coaching to address the identified key issues. In the story, Samuelsson ultimately decides to focus less on the money and more on building individual relationships with employees.

Step Three—Goal Setting and Accountability

The common wisdom about goal setting is that you get what you aim at. According to most studies in this field, 90 percent of laboratory and field activities that involved specific, articulated, and demanding goals resulted in better performance than activities with easy or no goals. In education, setting goals, and more specifically behavioral objectives, is critical to accomplishment—for both students and teachers. Thus, setting challenging but reasonable goals and objectives up front for both coach and client is necessary to stimulate progress, measure results (accountability), and manage expectations of everyone involved in the coaching process, including stakeholders. Typically, behavioral objectives consist of the action to be taken, a standard of performance, the timing of the action, and finally, the reporting of the results.

Following interviews with the client and a comparison of the client's and the stakeholders' observations on the 360 Continue-Stop-Start review (or other 360 evaluations available), the client sets personal goals and objectives to help guide him or her toward making a tangible and measurable plan. This typically takes one or two meetings, which are devoted to this process almost exclusively, with the client doing considerable work between the meetings. Primarily, I ask clients to reality-check their proposed goal(s) and objectives with the stakeholders who participated in the 360 evaluation or informal interviews.

Sharing goals and specific objectives with stakeholders before setting off to achieve them accomplishes several purposes:

- The clients let stakeholders know that they appreciate their input and value their opinions.

- It places outside (public) pressure on the clients to live up to now publicly stated goals.

- It gains moral and corporate support that helps the clients reach the goal. When your boss and friends know you're working hard to improve, they want to support your efforts—especially if early on (when you asked for their help), they had a hand in helping steer you in that direction.

In the story, Jane Smithfield and J.C. have an extended chat over several weeks to help nail down the objectives she would like to accomplish. Notice in the text that this is not a simple task, but rather a challenging process between coach and client. Setting objectives is difficult because it's about coming to grips with how you see your behavior and how others see you as well, and about your willingness to chart a new (unknown) course to change things.

After dialogue between J.C. and Jane, she decides to focus on better internal communications and on strategic thinking, because these objectives fit the company's most pressing need for her to grow into the CEO position. Eventually, she'll have to also tackle the communicating externally objective as well, but having clients focus on one or two objectives at a time is plenty, especially given their busy schedules.

When J.C. works with Jane Smithfield, you see a good example of how behavioral objectives are set and tracked. You may recall that, among other things, Jane wanted to improve her internal communications. With J.C.'s help and Jane's efforts, she constructed a very precise set of objectives that both she and J.C. could use to measure her progress—including when she had achieved her goals and objectives.

Step Four—Action Learning and Execution

Executing the plan, goals, and objectives is the guts of coaching. It's the period of three to six months of chipping away at each of these on a day-to-day basis. It's not glamorous or, for that matter, easy. And the payoff doesn't come right away—nor is it nearly as dramatic as the discovery phase or the goal-setting phase. If a good life is doing what you say, this is clearly the doing part. The execution phase is slower and cumulative. But over time, momentum and accrual of interest earned from daily deposits in this plan pay off in big, breakthrough dividends.

Thus, each couple of weeks, Jane Smithfield and all of the other clients will report their progress toward their goals and objectives to J.C. Often clients keep logs or journals to record daily activities. Others use an electronic document to simply record their activities that they then can tally each month. To illustrate, when Jane meets with a coworker, her journal entry might be: "Met with Jack Smith for 15 minutes on Tuesday, January 12th. We discussed the software engineering project he was working on and his one-year-old son, Ray. Jack had a picture of Ray and his wife, Nancy, on his desk."

Also, during this phase, it's very important for the client to get information from key stakeholders about the progress that the client is making. In the words of master coach Marshall Goldsmith, it's "feedforward" — getting information on how you can improve on specific behaviors in the future by people who have a strong interest in your success. Such feedforward information differs from feedback, which is typically about the past and often about mistakes that were made. Whereas, feedforward (or what I call "fast-forward" in the story) is a way of looking toward what the client can do to improve in the future, rather than ruminating about past failures or missteps.

Typically, I ask clients to start by talking to the same people who offered information on the 360 evaluation. Absent a 360, I ask clients to choose stakeholders above, below, and on the same level as they are, and to use such stakeholders as sounding boards. Clients check in with stakeholders every few weeks to ask for advice (never to argue or debate) and to thank them for their continued interest. It's important for clients to simply listen to what the stakeholder says they should do and keep the conversations as one-way as possible — the client listening to stakeholders and always thanking them. Likewise, it's important for stakeholders not to be cynical or sarcastic and to genuinely have an interest in the client's success, which they typically do — especially if they've been chosen by the client. In this process, there is usually a mutual respect that leads to progress.

Much "action learning" takes place during this phase of coaching. One example can be found in the chapter where Ann Tabor and J.C. actually role play in order to prepare her for her confrontation with Brad, the marketing executive who did not get the promotion he expected. You may recall that Ann and J.C. each played both roles to get the value of perspective from both points of view — Ann's and Brad's. Action learning may involve researching, testing, rehearsing a skill, or whatever it takes to get to the desired results.

Of all the stages, this one is the least sexy, yet most important. Doing the work to make the change is slow, tough, and, at times, a bit like walking or running uphill. Often, at the initial meeting with clients, I draw them a sketch of a graph with a ☺ at the top of the Y-axis and a ☹ at the bottom of that axis; then along the X-axis I draw a line with about six to twelve hash marks. The hash marks represent the months, and I show them that after several months they will hit a low point, which I call Death Valley.

This time frame seems to be the typical point where people "stall out." In the midst of this execution period, things aren't as interesting as they were in the discovery phase, and it just requires "doing stuff." I call this graph the Adaptation Cycle (see next page), because it's the way people adapt to change, even when they think it will be a good thing like getting a new job, or getting through the first year of college or the first year of marriage, or going through any life event requiring adaptation and change.

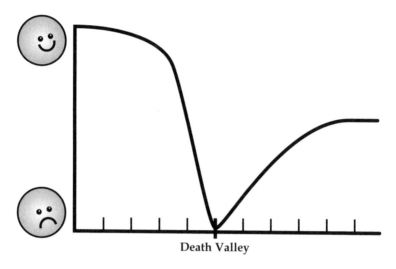

Death Valley

Adaptation Cycle

When I sense a client beginning to go through Death Valley, I pull out my original graph that I drew when we first started and ask, "Remember this?" They will vaguely nod. We have a pep talk, and basically I ask the client to buck up for another month. At this point, some people do and some don't—that's the reality of it. The ones who do push through make enormous strides. The ones who don't buck up, don't make as much progress. Some will even give up coaching, just like some kids drop out of college during the middle of their first year.

One of the gifts of this period of execution is that issues and challenges always crop up—issues that clients wish to discuss with me as their sounding board. My job is to provide support and insight as a thoughtful partner to help them solve the day-to-day challenges but then link those issues back to the overall goals we're working on.

Step Five: The Evaluation and Revision Phase

How will we know success when we see it? This is a key coaching question. If the coach has done a good job and the client has worked hard along the journey, we will have "Aha!" moments along the way. These are the times when clients look at something they've discovered and literally slap their own foreheads—as if they were seeing clearly for the first time in years.

When this happens, I always stop and congratulate them—to celebrate these special moments. I do this to recognize the client's hard work getting there, and I note it for my final report. We both need to remember the moment a client discovers why he or she has had such difficulty getting through to a board member, overcoming procrastination, quelling a temper, finding time to work on a strategic plan, taking a stand on innovation, or just deciding it's time to move on. These breakthrough or "Aha!" moments are the absolute gold of the coaching process. Recognizing and celebrating them when they happen documents the success and impact of coaching.

You must remember that making even a small but significant change is difficult—especially for people who have been successful. Typically, high achievers have been successful—they think—because of certain patterns of behavior. Those patterns might include abusive behavior, bullying, and anger tantrums, all of which might get short-term results but ultimately become incredibly derailing for these executives—especially as they climb the leadership ladder and begin to touch greater numbers of people. Thus, what might have worked before is inoperative now. However, successful people become almost superstitious about behavior (they think, *if it worked then, it will work now*). So like baseball players who get up to bat, these leaders adapt the same sort of rituals every time they face a new issue. Thus, breaking this cycle may at first seem minor, but the long-term results are very substantial for both the individual executives and for their organizations. Small changes in highly influential people mean big changes in their organizations.

A powerful evaluation tool is a questionnaire given to the client's stakeholders. For example, one question could be "Has Joe made any progress on communicating his vision for this project to employees?" The answer can be a simple "yes" or "no." An open-ended version of this question—for example, "Describe just what Joe did to communicate his vision to employees"—invites people to comment and share their observations.

Adding a ratings scale (often called a "Likert" scale) is an excellent way to give an essentially qualitative evaluation a degree of quantitative measure (and is the kind used by Marshall Goldsmith). Using this method, you add numbers to a qualitative judgment, which is powerful to clients because it puts progress at a very specific level and shows clients just how far they have moved the dial. Ideally, though it happens infrequently, we should do both a pre- and post-evaluation. However, the way to easily show progress is to set the starting point at 0. Then stakeholder evaluators can express positive or negative progress from the starting point.

Recall in the text that J.C. showed Jane Smithfield the kind of grid he would use as one way to evaluate her progress:

1. Jane has shown concrete behavioral change when interacting with people inside the company more positively.

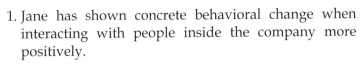

2. Jane has shown concrete behavioral change when interacting with people outside (external to) the company more positively.

At this point in the coaching process, we both may sense that the client is at a good stopping point—for whatever reason. If so, I provide a final report. Typically, I do this orally and will follow with a hard copy later. I use this period to recount the journey we've just taken together. I carefully review all the steps we took from our earliest pre-coaching meeting, to self-discovery and awareness, to goal setting and accountability, to action learning and execution, to evaluation and revision, so that the client remembers clearly every major twist, turn, bump, and straightaway we encountered from start to finish.

This technique has a remarkable effect on both the client and the coach. In a way, it's like looking at a scrapbook of a person's trip on vacation; as you turn each page, there's a smile, a laugh, a groan, even an occasional tear. So too, with this stage of the process—recounting the journey.

A key element of this stage of the process is acknowl-edgment and appreciation. It is a natural time to acknowledge how far the client has come—to have the client identify significant accomplishments of which he or she is proud. It is a time to express my own gratitude as the coach for the honor of helping that client on the journey. If it's apparent that further work needs to be done, we take this time to revise and/or develop new goals and objectives for the future, thus resetting the cycle until the client has accomplished his or her goals.

If the client elects to stop coaching, I ask: "So what did you think about the journey?" Responses are inevitably appreciative. Often, they have forgotten certain moments, perhaps minor events that later played out in a major way. I find this stage in the process both the highlight and the toughest phase. In a sense, it's like saying hello to a new person who has just come of age and saying goodbye to a friend at the same time.

Clients elect to stop coaching for any number of reasons—most of which are complex and unknowable—but for most, it's because they have attained their goals and have seen improvement in their work lives.

Final Words on Executive Coaching

I have been a teacher, mentor, and coach my whole life—whether in a classroom setting or as an executive mentoring someone in the workplace. I can't think of a better profession because it allows a person to give back a portion of what he or she has been given over the years. My appreciation and gratitude for my own journey have led me naturally to teaching.

And teaching has naturally led me to executive coaching. As I grow older, I realize two things: (1) that my own days of opportunity to positively change the world become fewer in number, and (2) that leaders have enormous power, especially at the highest levels of an organization. Given those factors, I made a conscious decision to focus on the highest levels of organizations—on CEOs and C-level executives—because a one-degree change in how they perform can have a huge impact on the rest of the organization.

When I talk to Human Resources officers or corporate executives to try to explain precisely what executive coaching is and how it works, I often ask them this: "Can you think of one thing your boss does that, if you could change it overnight, would make a dramatic change in the company?" I have never found an instance where the person didn't answer "yes," with a smile that implies absolute agreement. Fertile ground for this important work, indeed.

Best of luck in your own journey.

References

Buckingham, M., & Clifton, D. (2001). *Now, discover your strengths* (New York: The Free Press).

Gladwell, M. (2005). *Blink: the power of thinking without thinking* (Boston, MA: Back Bay Books).

Goldman, D. (1995). *Emotional intelligence* (New York: Bantam Dell).

Goldsmith, M. (2007). *What got you here won't get you there* (New York: Hyperion).

Johnson, S., & Blanchard, K. (1998). *Who moved my cheese?* (New York: Putnam Adult).

Lencioni, P. (2002). *The five dysfunctions of a team* (San Francisco, CA: Jossey-Bass).

Whitworth, L., Kimsey-House, K., & Sandahl, P. (1998). *Co-active coaching* (Mountain View, CA: Davies Black).